PRAISE FOR

LIVES GUIDED BY HONOR

"Lives Guided by Honor completely undresses Virginia Military Institute to the shirt stays and high black socks. Mayling Simpson gives an honest examination of VMI. All readers—whether a potential cadet, an alumnus, or a parent—can benefit from this white glove inspection. As part of the second class of women to attend VMI, I had my own love affair with the institute, one that leaves bruises and scratch marks. Questioning one's sanity in choosing this type of college is a normal part of being a rat in the Rat Line! Now more than ever, we need warriors, individuals with integrity, discipline, honesty, and perseverance to stand up for our country. With an education system that is weakening our teens with propaganda and dumbing down our society, the need for institutions like VMI has only grown. Warriors have to be made, and VMI is making them one sweat party at a time. *Lives Guided by Honor: How VMI Shaped the Class of 1968* reveals the secret ingredients to why strong traditions at VMI have remained for almost two hundred years and the influence society has had on the school to change with the times. I highly recommend."

—**Destiny Jennifer Ringgold,** author of *Choosing the Harder Right: West Point's 1976 Cheating Scandal.*

"Simpson has drawn back the veil to reveal this legendary and mysterious Southern institution. The writing style, subject presentation, and well-crafted structure kept me engaged with the subject, which, otherwise, could have been a very dry reading experience. She recognized that VMI was a very different educational experience than for most college students. For this reason, the only way for an outsider to understand and appreciate the stories of the Class of 1968 was to provide context. This required her to present a history of VMI and the evolution of its institutional culture. VMI alumni, historians, and American history buffs would be interested in this book. For a potential VMI applicant, I would say that this book would be an excellent source for understanding the culture of VMI. Indeed, a seventeen-year-old who would take the time to read this excellent portrait might have what it takes to be a successful cadet. Overall, the book is a significant contribution to American history."

—**James Gallager, MSc.**, geologist

"In *Lives Guided by Honor: How VMI Shaped the Class of 1968*, Mayling Elizabeth Simpson navigates the complex terrain of VMI's past as readers witness the profound impact of the institution's strict honor code and unwavering ethics on the graduating Class of 1968. Simpson skillfully weaves together personal narratives, institutional evolution, and societal shifts, creating a compelling narrative that goes beyond the walls of VMI. *Lives Guided by Honor* is a thought-provoking exploration of how an institution, rooted in traditions, can evolve, inspiring its graduates to lead lives of honor and integrity and contribute meaningfully to a diverse and inclusive society. I loved reading this book!

—**Dagny McKinley**, author of *Perry-Mansfield Performing Arts School & Camp: A History of Art in Nature, The Springs of Steamboat: Healing Waters, Mysterious Caves and Sparkling Soda*, and *The Adventures of a Girl & Her Dog*

"As a proud member of VMI Class of 1983, I really enjoyed this march down memory lane of what it means to be an honorable VMI graduate. Highly recommended!"

> —**Lynn Seldon, VMI Class of 1983**, author of *Virginia's Ring, Carolina's Ring*, and many other books

"A well written and thorough representation of VMI and our class. I learned so much about the history of VMI that I never knew. I cherish my time and the leadership, discipline, and especially the honor that VMI instilled in me. I depended on it as a twenty-four-year Air Force fighter pilot and leader. I referred to VMI and my experiences in my own books.

> —**Dana Duthie, Colonel, USAF (Ret), VMI Class of 1968**, author of *Dark Rain, Tremble, Phantoms of the Shah*, and *Convoy Cover*."

"Mayling Simpson's *Lives Guided By Honor* is a thoughtful, balanced, and well-researched work on the history of not only VMI but Virginia and the United States as a whole. A consequential work that addresses controversial issues during turbulent times in American history."

> —**Dave Rowland,** author of *Green Light, Go! The Story of an Army Start-up*

"*Lives Guided by Honor* is a beautiful gift to the VMI family—current and future: an expansive view of this venerable institution through a lens that ultimately focuses on the lives of the Class of 1968.

I was captivated by how the book describes the grounds, monuments, and art at VMI and its powerful cultural values in rich historical context—culminating with their lasting impact on the Class of 1968.

"This book shows that discipline and honor and the Rat Line are just as relevant today in shaping lives as they were throughout nearly two-hundred years of VMI's history.

I have not read a better analysis of the impact of organizational values on people. The accounts of monumental historical events and how they were experienced by students and faculty of VMI really light up the pages of this book.

No question in my mind, if I were looking for a college, *Lives Guided by Honor* would make me want to be a part of the special place that is VMI.

This is a book that captures the body and spirit of VMI. I can imagine it will accompany VMI admissions officers everywhere."

—**Kenneth B. Perkins,** provost emeritus and emeritus professor of sociology, Longwood University.

"A deeply personal account of the enduring impact of the Virginia Military Institute on members of the Class of 1968. Mayling Elizabeth Simpson has something important to say about the VMI community."

—**Bradley Lynn Coleman, PhD, VMI Class of 1995**, founder and senior historian, The Center for Applied History LLC

"Mayling Simpson's professional training as a cultural anthropologist and her personal experience with VMI bring objective insight into this very challenging, complex, and sometimes difficult-to-understand place. A commitment to personal Honor is the cornerstone of character development during a cadetship. Such commitment does not come easy and often brings serious reflection on how we choose to live our lives. The experiences of members of the VMI Class of 1968 are a testament to that commitment and the profound difference it makes. I particularly benefited from the insight I received from reading the personal stories of members of the class, several of whom I have known and admired for years."

—**Keith E. Gibson, colonel, VMI Class of 1977,** director VMI Museum System, author of *Virginia Military Institute*

"Mayling Simpson has captured the salient points about VMI.... Its adversarial Rat Line and single-sanction honor code create the most egalitarian collegiate educational system in the United States. Through good, bad, and ugly, the lessons learned at VMI have enabled its graduates to succeed in life. While we do not always agree with each other (or the author), we, the graduates of the Class of '68, are intimately bound together as the closest of friends, Brother Rats."

—**Dean Kershaw, Colonel, US Army Retired, VMI Class of 1968**

Lives Guided by Honor:
How VMI Shaped the Class of 1968

by Mayling Elizabeth Simpson

© Copyright 2024 Mayling Elizabeth Simpson

ISBN 979-8-88824-210-0

All rights reserved. No part of this publication may be reproduced, stored in a retrieval system, or transmitted in any form or by any means—electronic, mechanical, photocopy, recording, or any other—except for brief quotations in printed reviews, without the prior written permission of the author.

Published by

3705 Shore Drive
Virginia Beach, VA 23455
800-435-4811
www.koehlerbooks.com

LIVES GUIDED BY HONOR

How VMI Shaped the Class of 1968

MAYLING ELIZABETH SIMPSON

VIRGINIA BEACH
CAPE CHARLES

TABLE OF CONTENTS

Timeline 1

Superintendents 4

Author's Note 5

Foreword 7

Introduction 11

The Post 17

The Yankee in Me 21

Cadet Life 25

The Class of '68 40

John VanLandingham 51

The Prelude 69

Founders 85

Davis—The Architect 90

The Civil War Period 97

Post-Civil War Memorials 106

The Turbulent 1950s and '60s 117

Photos 127

The 1960s—A VMI Turning Point 136

A Theme of Honor Through Life 143

Creigh Kelley 152

The Best and Worst of Life 174

Class of '68 Advice to Future Cadets 181

Paul Hebert 189

Class of '68 Advice to the Institute 209

Afterword 216

Remarks to the Fiftieth Reunion 221

Acknowledgments 235

Bibliography 237

Endnotes 239

Survey Questions 245

TIMELINE

★ ★ ★

EVENTS INFLUENCING THE FOUNDING OF VMI

1755—Major George Washington named commander of all Virginia militias.

1776-1783—America's war of independence from Great Britain.

1778—The Virginia General Assembly passes an act to establish a "School of Instruction in the Art of Artillery and Fortification" and an arsenal for storing munitions.

1778—The town of Lexington, Virginia, incorporated.

1794—L'École Polytechnique founded in Palaiseau, France.

1802—United States Military Academy founded in West Point, New York.

1812—United States government declares war on Great Britain.

1816—Governor of Virginia asks citizens of Lexington to find a location for an arsenal.

1818—The Lexington Arsenal constructed.

1820s-30s—State of Virginia hires Claudius Crozet to design roads, bridges, and canals.

FOUNDING OF THE VIRGINIA MILITARY INSTITUTE

1834—The Franklin Society in Lexington recommends a military institute at the Lexington Arsenal on the plan of the West Point Academy.

1835—J. L. Preston publishes articles in Lexington Gazette advocating a military school.

1836—Virginia General Assembly passes an act to convert the Lexington Arsenal into a military school.

1837—The governor appoints a Board of Visitors (Crozet, Preston, Barclay, Leyburn, Dorman) for the new military school.

1839-40—VMI opens with twenty-eight cadets.

1849—VMI hires architect Alexander Jackson Davis to design new buildings.

1850—VMI begins construction of Old Barracks.

1856—Bronze statue of George Washington added on post.

1858—VMI admits students from outside of Virginia.

CIVIL WAR PERIOD

1859—VMI cadets attend the execution of John Brown in Charles Town, Virginia.

1864—VMI cadets fight for the South in the Battle of New Market (May).

1864—VMI post burned by Union forces (June).

1864-65—VMI post rebuilt led by Superintendent Francis H. Smith.

1865—Former Confederate officer John Mercer Brooke joins VMI faculty.

1865—Former Confederate officer and son of Robert E. Lee, G. W. Custis Lee, joins VMI faculty.

1868—Former Confederate Matthew Fontaine Maury joins VMI faculty.

MEMORIALIZATION OF THE CIVIL WAR

1878—VMI establishes a cadet cemetery for those who died in the Battle of New Market and the annual New Market Parade & Ceremony every May 15.

1896—West entrance to Old Barracks named after Thomas "Stonewall" Jackson.

1896—The first Jackson Memorial Hall built and the *Battle of New Market* painting unveiled in 1914.

1903—Bronze monument of *Virginia Mourning Her Dead* added on post.

1912—Bronze statue of General Stonewall Jackson added on post.

1916 —The second Jackson Memorial Hall built, and the *Battle of New Market* painting relocated.

MEMORIALS TO COCKE, SMITH, AND MARSHALL

1928—Memorial Garden constructed, a gift from Anne Cocke.

1931—Bronze statue of General Francis H. Smith added on post.

1939—Anne Cocke donates the Spirit of Youth statue to sit in Memorial Garden.

1949-51—"New Barracks" built and arch named for George C. Marshall.

1964—George C. Marshall Museum and Library added on post.

VMI BEGINS TO CHANGE FOCUS

1965—Jonathan Daniels, Class of '61 valedictorian, murdered.

1968—VMI admits five African American cadets.

1978—Bronze statue of George C. Marshall added on post.

1997—VMI admits female cadets.

1998—VMI establishes the Jonathan Daniels Humanitarian Award.

2004—Jonathan Daniels Arch named on west side of Old Barracks.

2006—Jonathan Daniels Courtyard added on post.

2008—"Third Barracks" completed, along with a new Lejeune Hall for cadet services.

2009—Marshall Hall with Hall of Valor and Center for Leadership and Ethics completed.

RECKONING WITH CIVIL WAR MEMORIALS

2020—Superintendent General Binford H. Peay III resigns amid Jackson statue controversy.

2020—VMI removes the Thomas "Stonewall" Jackson statue.

2021—VMI removes the name Stonewall Jackson from buildings.

2021—General Cedric T. Wins appointed first African American Superintendent of VMI.

SUPERINTENDENTS

★ ★ ★

Frances H. Smith, 1839-1889, US Military Academy, Class of 1833
Scott Shipp, 1890-1907, VMI, Class of 1859
Edward W. Nichols, 1907-1924, VMI, Class of 1878
William H Cocke, 1924-1929, VMI, Class of 1894
John A LeJeune, 1929-1937, US Naval Academy, Class of 1888
Charles E. Kilbourne, 1937-1946, VMI, Class of 1894
Richard J. Marshall, 1946-1952, VMI, Class of 1915
William H. Milton Jr., 1952-1960, VMI, Class of 1920
George R. E. Shell, 1960-1971, VMI, Class of 1931
Richard L Irby, 1971-1981, VMI, Class of 1939
Sam S. Walker, 1981-1988, US Military Academy, Class of 1946
John H. Knapp, 1989-1995, VMI, Class of 1954
Josiah Bunting III, 1995-2002, VMI, Class of 1963
J. H. Binford Peay III, 2003-2020, VMI, Class of 1962
Cedric T. Wins, 2021-, VMI, Class of 1985

AUTHOR'S NOTE

⋆ ★ ⋆

In 2018, I conducted a survey of the Virginia Military Institute's Class of 1968 to learn about their lives post-VMI. Most of the questions were open-ended, meaning they could write whatever they wanted rather than ticking a box. I asked why they attended VMI, what they did after graduation, when they married, what were their careers, what were the best and worse things that happened to them, and their advice to future cadets and the Institute. I asked no questions about the VMI Honor System.

Yet when the responses came back, they were filled with replies about how the VMI Honor System had shaped and affected their lives. I was emotionally overwhelmed as I read their words. Without asking about the Honor Code and VMI's single-sanction system (once you break the code, you are out), this is what they mainly wrote about. This was the thing that most influenced their lives. The latter part of *Lives Guided by Honor* summarizes the amazing wisdom shared by the Class of 1968, the core purpose of this book. I think you will agree that it is in the interest of our national security to produce men and women of such integrity to look after our country.

Before you get to those chapters, I give some background on cadet life and put VMI in the context of Virginia and national history. I touch on its founding, what the founders wanted to achieve, and the changes at the Institute over nearly 200 years. Without this context, my concern was that these men's words would fall flat. Especially for readers who know little to nothing about VMI, I needed to fill in that blank. The Institute has evolved over the years in tandem with the rest of the country. Cadets were and still are influenced by their surroundings both within the Institute and our wider world.

FOREWORD

★ ★ ★

"Higher education has never been terrifically good at measuring its impact," stated *Inside Higher Ed*. Yet, Dr. Mayling Simpson shows the lifetime impact of the Virginia Military Institute in *Lives Guided by Honor: How VMI Shaped the Class of 1968*.

Dr. Simpson sought to do a critical study of VMI and not a promotion of it. The book includes a tough look at its academics, adversative character development, history, culture, and VMI during the turbulent 1960s. The study led Dr. Simpson to conclude, "What I think makes VMI unique is its strong emphasis on honor, discipline, and brotherhood, a combination not necessarily found in other colleges."

This finding and others were based on data—and therein lies the book's great value. In 2018, Dr. Simpson initiated a survey of the surviving members of VMI's Class of 1968, with 121 or 44 percent responding. The findings are significant.

Overwhelmingly, the Class of 1968 respondents reported that their lives were profoundly influenced by VMI's Honor Code: "A cadet will not lie, cheat, or steal or tolerate those who do." Respondents attributed their adherence to the Code, to the "single-sanction." Violation means dismissal, with no second chances. For cadets coming from a world where the meaning of honor has varied, the single sanction enabled a realization that "there is only one kind of honor," said one class member.

Research has also shown that cheating is a slippery slope. "Once people behave dishonestly, they are able to morally disengage, setting off a downward spiral of future bad behavior and ever more lenient moral codes," concluded the study, "Dishonest Deed, Clear Conscience: When Cheating Leads to Moral Disengagement and Motivated Forgetting."

By comparison, Class of 1968 respondents showed an evolution in moral reasoning that went beyond concerns over personal consequences. Those experiencing combat—over half the Class of '68—saw honesty as a matter of life and death. Many echoed, "honor above self." One respondent said, "Live the VMI Honor Code. You may not be popular with all people, but you will be respected by those who matter." And "Without integrity, personal relationships fail, families fail, businesses fail, governments can fail, societies can fail," said another respondent.

Their words are indicative of Cicero's: "Within the character of the citizen lies the welfare of the nation."

Of equally great importance, the Class 1968 imparts wisdom for the VMI community to live by—which very much deserves reading from this graduate's perspective.

Some universities assess graduates' endeavors—and Dr. Simpson's findings address such metrics. Over 80 percent of respondents earned advanced degrees, including ones in law, medicine, and dentistry. An astonishing 98 percent said they were happy with their chosen professions, and nearly all said that VMI had prepared them for these professions.

Dr. Simpson does not hide the bad. Some respondents reported personal failures, which they attributed to straying from their values. Dr. Simpson also addresses the sufferings and misfortunes that the Class of '68 experienced—and that no one escapes.

While Dr. Simpson did not write a promotional book about VMI, from her writings emerged an admiration and tough love for it. Moreover, Dr. Simpson has done what few—if any—have done—provided a data-based approach for showing higher education's influence over a fifty-year lifetime, in this case, VMI's Class of 1968.

Dr. Simpson's methodology is one that VMI and other institutions should adopt, refine, and continually use to show evidence of higher education's value over their graduates' lifetimes.

Semper fi & VMI

—Thomas C. Linn '73

INTRODUCTION
A PARADE FOR THE CLASS OF '68

★ ★ ★

"Don't just speak your values;
live by them and show others that you walk the talk."
—A graduate, Class of '68

In April 2018, my husband and I stood along the edge of the parade ground at the Virginia Military Institute while the Cadet Corps of more than 1,700 men and women marched in honor of the fiftieth reunion of the Class of 1968. The student body of college-age men and women marched in perfect formation for forty-five minutes, in crisp, white uniforms, to a band of wind instruments, drums, and bagpipes. Cadet standard-bearers carried the American flag, the flag of Virginia, and the "New Market" flag (officially the VMI Regimental Flag).

Over a loudspeaker, an announcer called out the names of the companies and their cadet officers. The announcer, African American cadet Nathan Mumford, Class of 2019, said in his deep, commanding voice, "In 1966, the Class of 1968 marched in dedication of the fiftieth reunion of the Class of 1916."

That announcement really struck me. I thought to myself, *Wouldn't it have been interesting to know something about the lives of the men in the Class of 1916?* The Class of 1916, men born around 1898, may have served in World War I or II and probably lived interesting lives and held perspectives on how VMI shaped their lives. Those men would have been a little younger than our grandfathers, who were born in the early 1890s. As such, we could relate to the Class of 1916. Why *did* they attend VMI? What *did* they do with their lives after VMI? How many served in the military? What professions did *they* take up? And, importantly, what life advice might they have given the Class of 1968 if they had had the chance to share their thoughts after fifty years?

The reunion included luncheons and dinners and songs and chants in barracks that all current and former cadets knew. Everyone seemed so happy—graduates and current cadets alike. What were they so happy about?

For days following that parade, I kept thinking about the Class of 1916 and the Class of 1968. VMI graduates have a fierce loyalty to the Institute and its traditions. VMI goes out of its way to honor its graduates with impressive parades, beautiful dinners, and speeches. At the fiftieth reunion dinner, Superintendent General Peay gave a speech on the accomplishments of the Class of '68 and why 1968 was such an important year in US history. Other colleges have class reunions, but do they look like this? What is it about VMI that makes this happen?

I decided I wanted to do for the Class of 1968 what I wish someone had done for the Class of 1916: gather their reflections on how VMI had influenced them, what they had accomplished in life, what philosophies had guided their lives, and what advice they would give the current and future cadets. I also wanted to know whether the lives and accomplishments of the Class of 1968 were consistent with the intentions of VMI's founders in the 1830s. Does VMI produce the kind of graduates that the founders had in mind, or has there been significant change as society has changed?

In the summer of 2018, I sent a questionnaire to all surviving members of the Class of 1968, asking why they had attended VMI and how they lived their lives. I avoided questions about politics and religion. While the march on Charlottesville in August 2017 had occurred, the greater social upheavals of 2019 through 2020 had not yet occurred. There was a 44 percent response rate—121 men responded—which, in the survey world, is high.

The most striking feature of their answers was the important effect the VMI Honor System had on their lives. Their answers were often rich, but they were also anonymous. So, to bring to life these summarized responses, in 2022, I asked three 1968 graduates I knew to write brief life histories. John VanLandingham was president of the VMI Honor Court his senior year and went on to become a lawyer focusing on social justice. Creigh Kelley was a Vietnam veteran who pursued a career in running sports. My husband, Paul Hebert, applied his engineering training at VMI to a career in environmental engineering and United Nations humanitarian leadership. VMI selected him in 2011 to receive the Jonathan Daniels Humanitarian Award, and Paul later taught at VMI. If I had asked any other three men from that class, their stories likely would have been just as interesting.

Seven times over the past 183 years, VMI has made momentous decisions affecting its student body. 1968 was just one of those times. These decisions reflect the same struggles our country has experienced over the past 250 years—slavery, racism, and sexism.

The first of these events was VMI's decision at the request of Confederate Major General John C. Breckinridge, in May 1864, to send cadets, mostly teenagers, as reserve troops for the South during the Civil War in the Battle of New Market. That decision set VMI on a path to being identified with the Civil War, the Confederacy, and the Lost Cause narrative. The Lost Cause is "an interpretation of the American Civil War viewed by most historians as a myth that attempts to preserve the honor of the South by casting the Confederate defeat in the best possible light."[1]

Second, in 1912, was the erection of the statue of Thomas "Stonewall" Jackson, a Confederate general who had been teaching at VMI prior to the Civil War, at the head of VMI's parade field.

The statue was a culmination of veneration of Jackson that began in 1896, when the Jackson Arch was added to Old Barracks and Jackson Memorial Hall was built as a chapel and meeting hall.

The third decision was to shift the narrative of VMI graduates' heroic participation in the Civil War to their heroic participation in World War II. VMI collected WW II memorabilia from its graduates who had served, dedicated an arch to George C. Marshall, their famous VMI graduate, and erected two large bronze plaques listing the names of all VMI men killed in the war.[2]

Fourth was the admission of five Black cadets in 1968, a decision taken by Superintendent George Shell. This was VMI's first step toward racial integration with Black Americans. A fifth of Virginia's citizens were African Americans, but until 1968, Blacks had been excluded as cadets in this state-supported college.

Fifth was the admission of women as cadets in 1997 because of a Supreme Court decision, which I detail later. While this decision was thrust upon VMI, it was even more momentous than the admission of Black male students. The admission of women had seemed, up to this point, almost unimaginable.

Sixth was the establishment of the Jonathan Daniels Humanitarian Award in 1998 in remembrance of a 1961 graduate who was murdered in Alabama in 1965, following registering Black people to vote. This award repudiated racism and honored those whose lives were dedicated to equality and inclusion.

And seventh, in 2020, perhaps the most momentous shift in how the Institute was viewed from the outside, was the selection of VMI's first Black superintendent, General Cedric T. Wins, and the removal of the Thomas "Stonewall" Jackson statue, a decision made by the VMI Board of Visitors. The selection of General Wins signaled a shift away from the tradition of VMI being led by White males. The statue removal diminished VMI's symbolic tie to the Confederacy.

So, the Class of '68 represents one turning point in the history of the Institute.

To understand fully what these men said about how VMI influenced their lives, I describe the campus, cadet life, the social environment prior to the founding, the intentions of the founders, VMI's involvement in the Civil War, memorials after the Civil War, and the social and political environment of the era in which cadets in the Class of '68 were born and raised.

I am an anthropologist, a person endlessly curious about human beings and why they do what they do. While some people associate anthropology with stones and bones, that is, archaeology and paleontology, anthropologists are also trained to study contemporary cultures. We see culture as a continuum of past to present. VMI reflects the subculture of the American South through time. Anthropologists also explore the history of cultures they are studying, and I did so in this study. I also have the perspective of having been raised in both the North and the South.

I had been observing VMI over about five decades, beginning with visits for dances as a college student, being a "Ring Figure Ball" date, the formal event when 2nd Class cadets receive their class rings, and later accompanying my husband to class reunions, his award ceremony in 2011 (more on that later), living on post while he taught several semesters, and finally teaching there myself.

VMI's style of college education has intrigued me ever since my husband enrolled there in 1964. I could not imagine why anyone would want to spend their college years in military life (aren't you supposed to have fun in college?) unless they wanted a career in the military. And if so, why not go to a federal military training institution rather than one funded, in part, by the state of Virginia? Why on earth was VMI created to produce military officers when West Point already existed?

VMI alumni have an amazing lifelong comradery, and VMI maintains a strong direct relationship with its alumni through publications and year-round events. It's a college that has maintained its traditions and educational focus for over 180 years.

And so, something clicked in me when I attended my husband's fiftieth class reunion. It was at that moment that I decided to seek answers to the questions that had swirled in my head for so many years: the origin of VMI, the intention of the founders, and whether there was anything special about its graduates.

THE POST

* ★ *

"We shape our dwellings, and afterwards our dwellings shape us."
—Winston Churchill

Virginia Military Institute is a four-year military college in Lexington, Virginia, founded in 1839. Its student body today is comprised of about 1,700 students, of which about 12 percent are women and 6 percent are African American. It was founded as an institution to train young White men to be engineers, teachers, scientists, and military officers for the Virginia militia, an institution as old as the Jamestown settlement.

VMI was established on the site of a Virginia militia arsenal that had been built to store arms from the War of 1812 and then converted into a college. It was a time when people in the western part of Virginia were seeking political recognition from the Virginia State Assembly and lobbying for the right for all White men over twenty-one to vote, rather than just large landholding aristocrats. VMI would produce young citizen-soldiers who would be educated leaders for western Virginia. In 1964, when the Class of 1968 matriculated, the Institute was 125 years old.

The student body had grown from 28 students in 1839 to 1,200 by 1964. To accommodate this growth, the campus, called "post," had expanded from a single barrack, called Old Barracks, built between 1850 and 1924, to a second barrack, called New Barracks, completed in 1949. Other buildings, monuments, and statues had also been added along the way, but the founding traditions, uniforms, educational purposes, and military training had not changed much for more than 100 years.

Entering through VMI's main gate today, a scene of stoic serenity opens before you: cadet barracks, in three large, connected buildings with crenelated roofs and other Gothic Revival buildings, facing a large oval parade ground. From 1912 until December 2020, a bronze statue of Confederate General "Stonewall" Jackson stood in command at the far end of the parade ground, surrounded by four cannons on red carriages.

In 1968, the Jackson statue was clearly the center of post, the first impression the visitor got of VMI, the statue that all first-year cadets were required to salute when entering or leaving barracks. Barracks form a slight concave curve and have three front entrances and one back entrance. Each front entrance has an arch and a statue in front of the arch. The center arch was dedicated to Stonewall Jackson. To the right stands a statue of George Washington opposite the Washington Arch. To the left is the Marshall Arch, and in front of this arch is a statue of George C. Marshall, VMI's most famous graduate. The back entrance to the oldest barracks is dedicated to Jonathan Daniels. While there is no statue of Daniels, the Institute created the Daniels Memorial Courtyard just below the arch, displaying a plaque with his cadet picture and a summary of his death. Another plaque displays the names of all who received the Jonathan Daniels award.

These statues and arches form a kind of blueprint of the history of VMI, starting with the Washington Arch, so named in 1896, followed by the Jackson Arch in 1896, the Marshall Arch in 1951, and the Daniels Arch in 2004. Each arch and statue leads down a path of wanting to know more. Following those paths, they guide you through the changes that VMI has experienced over the decades, from its earliest visions to produce citizen-soldiers, through the turbulent years of the Civil War and the legacy of the Confederacy, followed by pride over its alumnus George C. Marshall, and finally its post-Lost

Cause awakening, with the sacrifice of alumnus Jonathan Daniels, who died for civil rights. But more on all this later.

This fortress-like campus and its parade ground with cannons shout a clear military mission of order, discipline, and seriousness, while the quiet olive beige of the buildings lends a peaceful atmosphere to the campus.

This whole opening scene at VMI, with its mix of Gothic and military symbols, is jarringly different from the Greek Revival architecture of Washington and Lee University, sitting just adjacent to VMI. W&L's red brick buildings, constructed between 1824 and 1842, have majestic white Tuscan columns that form a continuous line from building to building atop a hill. The two architectural styles, both popular in the early 1800s, stand side by side like a comparative study in the philosophy of architecture. Passing through Washington and Lee University, you might think of Plato and Aristotle and the Greek culture that brought us the works of Homer, as well as the balance and beauty of its architecture. Walking into VMI's medieval Gothic Revival post, you are overcome by a sense of solemnity, like something really serious is happening there.

On the surface, Virginia Military Institute looks like one of the federal military academies* that seek to produce commissioned officers for our four branches of the military. But it is not. VMI is a state college with an ROTC† program required of all cadets. Today, graduates may or may not choose to become commissioned officers in the US military.

In the 1960s, VMI graduates were expected to take a commission in a US military branch unless a physical problem disqualified them.

---

* The federal military academies are US Military Academy in West Point, New York, the US Naval Academy in Annapolis, Maryland, the US Air Force Academy in Colorado Springs, Colorado, The US Coast Guard Academy in New London, Connecticut, and the US Merchant Marine Academy in Kings Point, New York.

† ROTC stands for Reserve Officer Training Corps.

The years of active duty required and the length of reserve officer commitment depended on the branch of service of the cadet's commission. The typical minimum requirement for a US Army commission was two years. In 1990, the Board of Visitors abolished mandatory commissioning, except for those on ROTC scholarships. Today, 50 to 60 percent of VMI graduates take a commission in a selected branch of the military.

Students at US military academies are nominated by a member of Congress or the vice president or president of the United States, while VMI cadets apply for admission. VMI seeks to have students from all around the state as well as out-of-state students. Tuition at US Military academies is free, but VMI is not free and not cheap. Tuition assistance is available through Virginia State Cadetships, US military branches, and academic, athletic, and need-based scholarships.

Like the US military academies, VMI instills time-honored values, such as honesty, integrity, good manners, and service to the country. Graduates say the values they learned at VMI have stuck with them throughout their lives. As one '68 graduate said, "It may seem trite, but these values hold true. They are necessary for a successful career, marriage, and life."

THE YANKEE IN ME

"To a foreigner, a Yankee is an American. To Americans, a Yankee is a Northerner. To Northerners, a Yankee is an Easterner. To Easterners, a Yankee is a New Englander. To New Englanders, a Yankee is a Vermonter. And in Vermont, a Yankee is somebody who eats pie for breakfast."
—American Author E. B. White

I n October 1964, I made my first trip to VMI to visit my high school sweetheart (and future husband), Paul Hebert, who had recently become a cadet. We had attended George Wythe High School in Richmond, VA, and had graduated the previous spring. I was a freshman at Longwood College in Farmville, Virginia, a women's college at that time. I had no idea what to expect and was surprised to see that VMI was built like a fortress and had a statue of Thomas "Stonewall" Jackson at one end of the parade ground. It felt just a bit like entering a different era. Behind the stage in Jackson Memorial Hall was an enormous painting of the Civil War Battle of New Market, where ten cadets had died defending the Confederacy. A beautiful bronze sculpture, *Virginia Mourning Her Dead,* sat protectively over the grave markers of the ten cadets who sacrificed their lives. The place looked to me like a memorial to the Confederacy.

There was a parade the day I arrived. Some 1,200 cadets—dressed in military uniforms, like those worn in the 1800s, carrying M1 rifles, with bayonets from World War II—marched in precise and impressive formation. A New Market Flag was waving alongside an American flag. I felt as though I had stepped back in time. I thought the Civil War was long gone, and even World War II, for me, seemed long ago, even though it had ended a mere nineteen years earlier. The contrast with Longwood College, with its Palladian-Jeffersonian architectural style and complete lack of Confederate symbols, was stark.

There is little doubt that I was looking at VMI through different eyes than the average Virginian. I had grown up in Ohio, and in the summer of 1960, when I was fourteen, my family moved to Richmond, Virginia, from Columbus during the height of racial unrest in Richmond and across the country. Indeed, cities across the US were burning that summer due to racial riots.

My Ohio home had been part of the Underground Railroad. The old house came with a barn full of nineteenth-century antiques and a small library of abolitionist literature, including a first edition (1855) copy of *My Bondage My Freedom* by Frederick Douglass, all of which I had read as a child. That experience, no doubt, had formed my opinions about slavery and the Civil War. My Kentucky ancestors had fought on both sides of that war, and my grandparents had passed down stories from that time. I quizzed my parents about this aspect of American history since our house seemed to be some sort of living museum from that era. As a result, the Civil War seemed very real to me.

I had been around the military all my life. My father had joined the Army in 1942, attended Officer Candidate School in Petersburg, Virginia, and became a second lieutenant. He was promoted to first lieutenant in Louisville, Kentucky, on the day of my birth in 1946. At that time, my parents were living in my maternal grandparents' upstairs apartment on their dairy farm outside of Louisville, a farm that had been in my grandfather's family since 1811. I guess you can say we were a Southern family. My relatives spoke with a Kentucky drawl. When I was six months old, my father, a civilian in the Army Reserve, took a job in procurement at the Department of Defense in

Columbus, Ohio. We lived in Columbus and, later, in the 1858 house in the nearby town of Reynoldsburg until I was fourteen. I remember my father dressing in his military uniform to attend Army Reserve meetings and going away for two weeks every summer to Army Reserve training. Over the years, he was promoted to captain, major, and eventually lieutenant colonel. In 1960, my father was offered the position of civilian director of the Defense General Supply Center in Richmond, Virginia, and we moved to Richmond. My parents were members of the Bellwood Officer's Club, and I remember my mother attending the Officer's Wives Club, smartly dressed in a suit, hat, heels, and white gloves. I remember my father receiving military and civilian awards.

However, our move to Richmond was my first culture shock. While my parents were Southerners, my upbringing had not been Southern. After a childhood in Ohio, I had to adjust to an entirely new culture, Virginia culture. And there, I saw firsthand the legacy of slavery: racial apartheid in schools, shops, buses, and restaurants. Jim Crow laws. I also learned about the Confederacy and the narrative of the Lost Cause, which was completely new to me. My parents took my two sisters and me to Monument Avenue in downtown Richmond to see the row of statues of Confederate leaders lined up in the wide green median strip between the two lanes. I remember how amazed and disturbed I was; I could hardly believe what I was seeing. I felt I was in a different country, one that still glorified those who fought to maintain slavery. Those monuments, erected between 1890 and 1930, were intended to remind people of a glorious Lost Cause of the Civil War. I had no difficulty connecting my historic home in Ohio to the riots and racism I was seeing in Richmond. Four years later, my first visit to VMI evoked emotions from my first summer in Richmond.

On that first visit, my cadet also looked different. He had lost perhaps twenty pounds. His face was thin, very pale, and drawn, and he looked tired. When he smiled, wrinkles formed around his eyes and down the sides of his cheeks, and he was only eighteen years old.

He looked like he had been "through the mill," as they say. Ground down. VMI had removed every ounce of fat from his football player physique. He introduced me to his four roommates, all of whom looked just as drawn and tired. He showed me his living quarters, his "hay" (bed) stacked against a wall of a crowded room on the fourth stoop of barracks—five beds, five rolled mattresses, five desk chairs, five worktables, five desk lamps, five wardrobes, five rifles.

I was no doubt dressed that day in a matching skirt and sweater set and leather flats, having carefully chosen my wardrobe for the weekend to look smart. I knew some other Longwood girls who were dating cadets at VMI, so I most likely had hopped a ride with another, probably older, Longwood student, as I had no car, and there was no public transport between Farmville and Lexington. Another interesting tidbit of that distant time is that our only access to telephones was the public pay phones in dorm hallways. We also had no access to televisions, refrigerators, or personal computers, all things standard in today's college dorms. Communication with our cadet friends was mostly by letter and somewhat through the single public phone on our dorm floor.

From 1964 to 1968, I traveled several times to VMI, usually with my classmates, to attend formal dances, parades, and other ceremonies. We stayed in Lexington, in bed-and-breakfast homes approved by VMI, at a cost of one or two dollars a night. The cadets made reservations for our stays, and we often shared double or triple rooms. I remember the turn-of-the-century brick house I usually stayed in and the upstairs bedroom and bath shared by four or five girls.

So, why were my cadet and his roommates looking so tired and stressed? Was it the uniforms? Was it the strict daily schedule? Was it being worn out from football practice? Were the academics too tough? Were they not getting enough sleep? It did not look like they were having fun in college (like I was!). So, what was going on?

CADET LIFE

*"If the VMI Honor Code were universally accepted,
our country and the world would be much better."*
—A graduate, Class of '68

What was happening to make rats (new cadets) look so tired was a very strict daily and weekly schedule that included not only fifteen to eighteen class hours per week but also many other exhausting activities. Cadets have at least three hours per week of military physical training that includes running, jumping over barriers, crawling under barriers, push-ups, sit-ups, pull-ups, climbing walls, and scrambling over rocks. Then there is early rising, before 7 a.m., forming up and marching to meals and, for rats, frequent harassment by upperclassmen that involves orders to do dozens of push-ups and to strain‡ while standing and at meals. Cadet athletes are exempted from much of ROTC physical training during the athletic calendar but have two hours per day of athletic practice, except on weekends when most scheduled games and meets occur. In short, nearly every minute of the weekday is scheduled, and much of it is required physical activity. Rats have the additional stress of just being a rat.

DAILY AND WEEKLY SCHEDULE

The daily and weekly schedule followed at VMI was nearly the

---

‡ Straining involves standing up straight with shoulders back and chin tucked as close to the chest as possible.

same in the 1960s as it is today. The Institute publishes operating rules of the Institute schedule, a daily and weekly guide outlining where all cadets are supposed to be at any time, Monday to Friday. The only free time during the weekday is 7:30-7:45 p.m., that brief interval between the end of supper and the beginning of study time. Saturday mornings are scheduled, including various other duties. Saturday afternoons and Sundays until 7:00 p.m. are free time.

According to institute documents, the intent of the daily and weekly schedule is "to provide guidance and a basic framework that facilitates Cadet success at VMI." The philosophy is that

> the Institute Schedule sets the tempo of the cadets' day according to a specific operational blueprint. It provides guidance identifying where the cadet will be and which activities are authorized to be scheduled (and by whom) during specific periods. Constructs such as Academic Class Periods, Dean's Time, Commandant's Time, Superintendent's Time, Evening Study Period, Dean's, ROTC's and Commandant's Saturdays, and the like are designed to fence blocks of time for specific activities, to discipline the members of the Institute against encroaching on others, and to add discipline, structure, and clarity to the cadet's life.

This operating guidance

> provides a schedule of events to balance a cadet's academic, athletic, military and life activities to participate in a full VMI experience and qualify for graduation. When a cadet is required to be at more than one place at the same time, it is incumbent upon the cadet to de-conflict the situation prior to that time—asking forgiveness for an absence after the fact is not an acceptable course of action. [3]

The weekday schedule, expressed in military time, begins Sunday at 1900 and ends at 2230 on Friday. Monday through Friday begins with reveille at 0700. All cadets (except for those involved in ROTC or athletic training, when start times may be one hour earlier) are required to form into their company units, and those wanting breakfast march in formation to the dining hall. New cadets are marched back to barracks after breakfast to receive instructions for the day. The midday meal is taken between 1100 and 1300, according to the student's own schedule.

Every evening, cadets fire a 105 mm howitzer, lower the American and Virginia State flags, and march by company to Crozet Hall for supper. Supper roll call (SRC) is at 1830, and all companies form. Those wishing to eat supper march to the dining hall as a unit. Rats need to return to barracks by 1930. The evening study period is 1945 to 2330 (2345 on Friday).

All cadets go through weekly physical training. On Mondays, all ROTC programs (Army, Navy, and Air Force) do physical training from 1600-1800. Cadets do additional training at 0600-0715 on Tuesday, Wednesday, or Thursday, depending on their branch of the ROTC program. Wednesday afternoons, weather permitting, are reserved for practice parades.

Classes are held Monday through Friday until 1600. Cadets may not miss a class unless excused by their instructors or due to injury or illness and have a doctor's note. The day ends at 2230 with Taps, a traditional military melody played on a bugle. During every part of the day, cadets are supposed to be in their "right" place. If a TAC§ officer discovers that a cadet is not in his or her right place at a certain time, the officer can assign demerits or penalty tours (marching in front of barracks in one-hour units). Cadets assigned penalty tours for infractions form up according to a weekly schedule to march off

---

§ A tactical officer (TAC) is a current or retired military officer or faculty member whose responsibility is to maintain discipline among the cadets. He can give demerits for breaking rules.

their penalties. Formal parades take place on Friday afternoons and Saturday mornings for events like awards, home football games, and for special visitors. The Class of '68 had to attend academic classes on Saturday mornings.

The only days cadets in the 1960s had for a little relaxation from the routine were Wednesday afternoons from 4:00 p.m. until SRC, Saturday afternoons, and Sundays when they could visit the town of Lexington for a meal or meet with family and friends. Cadets had few opportunities to leave the post for extended breaks, but permission for leaves increased as cadets moved upward from 4th to 1st Class cadets. National Collegiate Athletic Association (NCAA) athletes had increased privileges, more flexible times for meals, and time off before and following team competitions. However, athletes were given no academic breaks and were required to make up for any class time missed due to sporting events. Most of these rules are still true today.

THE THREE PILLARS OF VMI'S MILITARY TRAINING

Values have always been the core of a VMI education. You feel it when you visit the campus, the way students say, "Good morning, ma'am" and "Good evening, sir" to everyone they pass. They open doors for visitors and professors, and they attend their classes with punctuality. Lying, cheating, and stealing, it is said, are rare events. One '68 graduate said that if all the world lived by the values taught at VMI, the world would be a better place. So, how are these values instilled?

Colonel Dean Kershaw, Class of '68, now a part-time professor of civil engineering and TAC officer in his retirement under the Office of the Commandant, explained to me the importance of this system to the formation of disciplined individuals. He clarified that VMI's military training stood on three pillars: the discipline system, the Honor System, and the Rat Line. This is the system that has changed very little since the founding of VMI. This is the system that explains the weight loss, the eye bags, and the crying on the pillow at night.

THE DISCIPLINE SYSTEM

The first pillar is the discipline system. This system is intended to teach self-discipline—keep your room clean and tidy, yourself clean and tidy, your rifle clean, be where you are supposed to be always, follow orders, and do not break any rules. This is the same system used by all the military academies and military branches. It is essential for maintaining a disciplined military, ready for service when called. Soldiers and sailors must follow orders.

There are set penalties for the various violations described in a booklet called "The Blue Book," given to each cadet. The penalties are a three-tier stacked system, depending on the severity of the violation. The first tier is demerits. The second tier is penalty tours, and finally, the third tier is confinement to barracks, meaning one cannot leave the post. For example, a cadet could be disciplined with ten demerits, five penalty tours, and one-week confinement, or with just ten demerits and nothing else. An excessive number of demerits per semester (today, one hundred) results in suspension for the rest of the semester or the rest of the academic year. Suspension is so serious that it is a decision of the superintendent.

Demerits, restrictions to post, and penalty tours are assigned for infractions not so serious as to merit dismissal or suspension, and demerits alone are assigned for minor offenses. For the most part, demerits were given for things like a belt buckle not being shiny enough, a shirt not tucked in properly, shoes not shined, a rifle not clean, wearing the wrong uniform for the time of day or occasion, or being at the wrong place. An excessive accumulation of demerits is regarded as failure or inability to adjust satisfactorily to the military requirements and may result in suspension or dismissal.

Excessive demerits—or "offenses seriously subversive of high standards of character and conduct"—trigger temporary suspension from the Institute.[4] The VMI catalog describes those offenses like this:

> In the interest of good order and discipline, the Institute reserves the right to dismiss, suspend, or otherwise penalize any cadet who does not properly adapt to the life and work of the college. Among the offenses that are considered seriously subversive of high standards of character and conduct and, which may result in dismissal, are disobedience of orders, combinations against authority, hazing, uncivil or disorderly conduct, use or possession of alcoholic beverages within the limits of the Institute or in a way to bring discredit to the corps, absence without leave, habitual neglect of academic or military duty, and unauthorized use of explosives. Any use or possession of unauthorized illegal drugs or unauthorized possession, distribution, or use of prescribed drugs is a dismissal offense. Any conviction of an honor violation is a dismissal offense.

Despite the seriousness of the discipline system, some cadets try to buck the system in any way they can, just to see what they can get away with. For example, there is "running the block," which is leaving post at unauthorized times or being in unauthorized places on post, such as being on the fourth stoop, the rat stoop, if you are not a rat, or trying to sell items to rats (a vulnerable group, scared to say "no"). Selling anything to other cadets is not permitted.

THE HONOR SYSTEM

The second pillar is the Honor System. Cadets pledge not to lie, cheat, steal, or tolerate those who commit these acts. This system is intended to build trust. Cadets who violate the Honor Code are dismissed permanently from the Institute. This is called "drumming out." Cadets in the 1960s were summoned by loudspeaker in the middle of the night to gather around the stoops of the Old Barracks, where drums rolled, and the president of the Honor Court called out the name of the cadet being dismissed. It was an emotional and dramatic moment.

The guilty cadet was not present but had been taken to a hotel in town. The event made a lasting impression on all present. Today, the name of the cadet is not called out, but it is still an emotional event.

The Honor System at VMI is a single-sanction system, meaning there are no second chances. Cadets who make it through this system can be trusted to tell the truth always, no matter how difficult or embarrassing, never cheat, and never steal. "That means you can have confidence in anyone wearing the VMI ring," Colonel Kershaw explained to me. "It is like professional licensing of engineers. We license them to ensure the health and safety of the public. Will this bridge stand up? Can I cross it safely? The answer is yes if the design engineer was licensed. So it is with VMI graduates. We develop in them a moral compass that guides their professional and personal lives. It's all about building character," Kershaw emphasized. Would you want to go to a doctor or dentist who cheated on medical exams? Of course not. But how can you know? Colonel Kershaw says you can trust anyone of any profession who graduated from VMI. Period. Employers in Virginia know this, which is one reason VMI graduates are so readily employed at graduation.

THE RAT LINE

The third pillar is the Rat Line. The intention of the Rat Line is to erase every bit of status a new incoming cadet may feel he or she has. Were you the star football player in high school? The valedictorian of your class? One of the rich kids in school? God's gift to your high school? Son or daughter of an Army general, state senator, or former governor? If so, forget it! You are nothing now but a rat!

Making young people into rats is a bit like making gingerbread men out of dough. You beat them down, mix them up, and then cut them out all the same. Incoming rats have their heads shaved and are fitted into uniforms, all looking exactly alike. Their egos are beaten down, and their tolerance for harassment is toughened by hazing. If a rat looks different—hair color, freckles, or accent—that person will be mercilessly taunted. The Rat Line bonds the new class together, like Army basic training. That first year is not about *me* but about *us*, Colonel Kershaw explained. Brother rats become closer to each other than to their own family members. They suffered together and survived together.

Upon entering the corps, rats are given a pamphlet called *The Bullet*, better known as the "Rat Bible," and are expected to memorize all of it. I draw here from *The 2013 Bullet*, as the essential messages of *The Bullet* were the same in the 1960s.

The Bullet begins with a preface titled "TO THE RAT":

> Within your first five minutes at VMI you will realize that you have entered a new world, a world in which your previous system of values is neither valid nor influential. You will find yourself in a harsh world from which, at the end of two weeks, you may discover that a good number of your potential "Brother Rats" have departed. Upon matriculation you will be confronted with a great number of Institute rules and regulations, yet just as important as these, and in some cases more important to the Rat, are the rules that the Cadet Corps has chosen to impose upon itself; these rules are to be found in the policies of the Honor Court, the General Committee, and the Executive Committee. Even more perplexing to you will be the unwritten rules, adopted as tradition through the years, for the administration of the Rat Line. As a Rat it is your duty to learn these rules as soon as possible; this is a necessity, and ignorance of the rules constitutes no excuse in any manner.
>
> You are a Rat. It will take time for you to become accustomed to the appellation, yet the name is just; you are the lowest people in the Cadet Corps, you know nothing of the VMI system, and until you and your class have proven yourselves capable of accepting and carrying out the

responsibilities of a VMI Cadet, you will remain Rats. Many times during the year you will become discouraged; you may believe that the "Rat Line" has become unjust; you may feel as if you are being singled out without reason; and you may believe that the "Rat Line" has no other purpose than to allow upperclassmen to administer useless regulations solely for their amusement; however, this is all part of a system with definite long and short range purposes in mind. You must remember that those who administer the "Rat Line," from the superintendent to the Third Class private, have all received the same treatment.

Perhaps the most important aspect of your situation to keep in mind is that you Rats are the people who make VMI what it is; if it were not for the existence of the "Rat Line," VMI would be just another military school. This "Rat Line" is the heart of the military system; the physical and mental courage one stands to gain is that courage, which has distinguished VMI graduates as unique in all fields.

As you struggle with the demands of the Rat Line, be cognizant that enduring the Rat Line does not in and of itself herald success. Success as a Rat means that you are distinguished academically, militarily, and you have developed a high level of physical fitness. Above all, the successful Rat has accepted a code of conduct punctuated by honorable and ethical behavior that is the hallmark of all VMI graduates.

Chapter one of *The Bullet* is dedicated to "HONOR ABOVE SELF." Written as a letter from the Honor Court president, it explains the meaning of the Honor System:

> Rats,
> By matriculating at VMI, you have already portrayed a desire to set yourself apart from the rest of your peers and

take the adversative road to a college degree. To set out upon this path is not enough, it is a prolonged journey that you must commit yourself wholeheartedly to in order to reap the benefits of a VMI diploma. You are well aware of the flaws of our society in term of honesty, integrity, and moral fortitude. These shortcomings in moral character are not a part of VMI culture. The Honor Code states: A CADET WILL NOT LIE, CHEAT, STEAL, NOR TOLERATE THOSE WHO DO. It is this simple statement that not only bonds cadets with other cadets, but cadets with generations of alumni. Our system is supported entirely by the Corps of Cadets and without your strict adherence and adoption to the Code, it is nothing but meaningless charter on your wall. You will forget your old ways and live by the Code. From this moment on, you have the same degree of ownership and responsibility of upholding and enforcing our Code as the senior-most Firstclassman. Nowhere else in the country students live in unlocked dormitory rooms, take exams without the presence of an instructor, or take another peer's word as the whole truth. This is the system that lays the foundation for the entire VMI way of life. Take pride in our Code, embrace it, reap its benefits, and always place it before anything else at the Institute.

The Honor Code should guide your every action during your time not only at VMI, but also in every facet of your civilian life. To embrace our Code only during your cadetship would be a failure of the deeper meaning of the Honor Code. Our system is meant to serve as your ethical foundation to a life centered on integrity, honesty and a moral compass that will guide you through your life beyond the Institute. Our society is in desperate need of men and women who possess such character traits and have the moral courage to enact change on those around them. I challenge you to accept this undertaking; for the Institute, our alumni, family, friends, and society will accept nothing less than a wholehearted devotion to our cause. This is our Code and your chance to impart real changes on those around you.

Welcome to the Virginia Military Institute.

Importantly, the rat must memorize the VMI cadet code of conduct, written in *The Bullet* as follows

- ★ A cadet's word is their bond.
- ★ A cadet embodies integrity at all times.
- ★ Duty to country, state, corps, family and friends is sacred to a cadet.
- ★ A cadet offers equal respect, treatment, and understanding to all.
- ★ A cadet never takes advantage of the weaknesses of others, nor harms those who are unable to defend or assert themselves.
- ★ A cadet values their physical well-being.
- ★ A cadet displays habitual good manners, grace, and good humor.
- ★ A cadet is modest in dress, speech, and habits, displaying at all times behavior guided by high thoughts and plain living.
- ★ A cadet never takes counsel of their fear.

The Rat Bible states, "Without a strict observance of the fundamental Code of Honor, no person, no matter how 'polished,' can be considered well mannered. The honor of a VMI cadet demands the inviolability of word, and the incorruptibility of principles."[5]

The Rat Disciplinary Committee, composed of upperclassmen, is assigned the task of enforcing the Rat Line. They make sure rats are held to the highest fitness standards, conducting "sweat parties," marches, runs with rifles, and stadium workouts. It's really tough.

"Breakout" from the Rat Line usually occurs in February of the first year. After a hellish week of physical demands, rats are released from the Rat Line and henceforth referred to as 4th Class cadets. Even after the first year, life at VMI was and is still hard. There is no sleeping in during the morning. Mealtimes are fixed. There is a lot of marching, more marching, lining up, standing, and following a strict set of rules about how to dress, how to hold your body when walking or sitting, how to maintain shined shoes and short hair, and how not to laugh, even if you find some of this to be funny.

ACADEMIC MAJORS

When the Class of '68 attended VMI, the Institute offered majors in civil and electrical engineering, biology, chemistry, physics, history, English, mathematics, foreign languages (French, German, and Spanish), and economics, with classes held Monday through Saturday morning. Today, a few more majors are offered, including international studies (currently the most popular of all majors) and computer science, as well as a wide range of minors. Unheard of during the tenure of the Class of '68, cadets today have the opportunity to study abroad and learn a wider range of foreign languages, including Chinese and Arabic. To graduate, cadets must maintain a minimum 2.0 out of 4.0 grade point average. VMI has attained a high ranking among public liberal arts colleges in the United States. The Institute has produced eleven Rhodes scholars since 1921.

UNIFORMS

In the 1960s, upon matriculation, cadets were required to purchase a summer uniform[¶], which is called their "whites:" white shirts and white trousers; a winter uniform consisting of a black flight jacket, gray shirts, a short, gray wool tunic, called a "blouse," and gray wool trousers; and a formal uniform consisting of a coatee[**], with three

---

[¶] Today, cadets rent their uniforms.
[**] A coatee is a tight-fitting jacket short to the waist in front and short tails behind.

rows of vertical brass buttons, formal trousers with black stripes, and a tall hat, called a "shako," topped with a large black tassel. They purchased, in addition, an extremely impressive and handsome long, gray wool overcoat with a cape lined in red wool. They wore standard black military shoes. (Today, the female cadets have white skirts for summer formal wear.) For military training, cadets in the 1960s wore gray fatigues but today wear standard camouflage Army field uniforms. For physical training, they wear standard sweatpants, sweatshirts, T-shirts, and shorts. All these uniforms are prescribed according to time of year and activity. No cadet may wear any other type of clothing while on post or in Rockbridge County while the Institute is in session during the regular academic year. Summer school students are exempted from these clothing requirements.

BARRACKS

All cadets live in barracks. Barracks are interconnected by passages on each of the four levels, called "sally ports." Each barrack opens onto its own central courtyard. Rats occupy the fourth floor or stoop. The 3rd Class cadets occupy the third stoop, the 2nd Class the second stoop, and the 1st Class is on the ground level. The rooms vary in size and are occupied by three to five cadets each. Each cadet has a desk, chair, closet, and bed, called a "hay," which consists of a folding wooden bed frame and a mattress, stacked against a wall every morning and not put down until after supper.

INSPECTIONS

To teach cadets the importance of self-discipline and following orders and to ensure that they do so, the commandant's office has a cadre of twenty-five to thirty tactical officers who are assigned to cadet companies. They inspect cadets and their rooms, and they alternate duty as officer in charge, roaming barracks and post in the evening hours and making sure everything is in order. When a violation is spotted, such as needing a haircut, needing to shine shoes, or being in the wrong place, a TAC officer can tell a cadet to correct his or her behavior immediately and report back after correcting the behavior. If the cadet does not immediately correct the behavior, the TAC officer can place a cadet *on report*, which is called "being boned." That report goes to the commandant's office. The commandant determines the punishment for the violation.

In the 1960s, TAC officers also carried out "stick checks," starting at 10:00 p.m., tapping on room doors or other parts on post to see whether cadets were where they were supposed to be at a given time. Stick checks no longer occur. The 3rd Class cadets inspect rats who are standing in formation (by company) prior to supper roll call while TAC officers inspect upperclassmen. Any deficiencies in inspections or infractions of the rules result in being "boned."

During the 1960s, VMI prohibited cadets from drinking alcoholic beverages, even in restaurants. Today, cadets twenty-one years or older may drink alcohol in restaurants. Alcohol and drugs were, and still are, strictly forbidden in barracks, an offense that can result in suspension from the Institute.

Generally, life has always been challenging at VMI, especially for new cadets. It is not unusual for 10 percent of a new matriculating class to quit the corps before the end of the first semester, many by the end of the first two weeks. New cadets experience stress, sleep deprivation, and physical fatigue, and they learn perseverance and self-discipline in return. As so many graduates have said, VMI is not for everyone!

UPPERCLASSMEN

After rats "break out" from the Rat Line, they are known as 4th Class cadets. That is, they now need to work their way up the ranks to become 1st Class cadets and graduate. The 3rd Class cadets form the "cadre" tasked with disciplining all new cadets—rats.

The Institute holds four weekend dances during the year: homecoming, Ring Figure Ball, mid-winters, and spring formal.

Cadets wear their formal VMI military uniforms, and their dates wear formal clothing. When cadets reach their third year at the Institute, they receive their VMI class rings at a November formal dance and ceremony called the "Ring Figure Ball." This is one of the most important rites of passage at the Institute. In the past, when all cadets were males, they asked a young woman to attend the dance and present them with their class rings. The women traditionally wore white formal gowns, and the cadets wore their dress uniforms. Some men gave their Ring Figure date a pin that represented the ring or an actual small class ring. Today, the tradition is much the same, but the Institute has both male and female cadets who receive the rings from their respective escorts.

Becoming a 1st Class cadet, that is, a senior, confers new privileges to cadets—additional leave from post, serving as "dykes" to rats, serving in all the corps leadership positions, ability to become president of the Honor Court, and, in the 1960s, being editors of the newspaper, *The V.M.I. Cadet*,†† and the *Bomb* yearbook, among others. The 1st Class cadets look forward to graduation in the spring, where they receive their diplomas and federal military commissions for those who have chosen that route. Immediately after graduation, hats fly in the air, uniforms come off, graduates grab their "hay" to take home, and everyone leaves.

So, who elected to attend VMI in the 1960s, and why? The Class of '68 provides some answers.

---

†† *The V.M.I. Cadet* newspaper used to be a VMI-sponsored program, like the yearbook, the *Bomb*. But it was abandoned several years ago. In 2020, an alumnus offered to sponsor the newspaper, recruited several cadets, and began republishing . . . without VMI oversight. VMI objected to not having it organized as a cadet club and publicly disavowed the newspaper. It is now being published as an underground newspaper.

THE CLASS OF '68

★ ★ ★

"It has been fifty-four years since 368 of you signed the Matriculation Book and became VMI cadets. . . . It marked the beginning of VMI's 125th year. . . . For most of the rest of the year, you were known to the upper classes as 'the rat mass.' It would be some very long months of testing, and not until nearly the end of the academic year did you become 'the fourth class,' the 'Class of 1968.'"
—VMI Superintendent General J. H. Binford Peay III,
April 2018, fiftieth class reunion

On September 10, 1964, parents and relatives from all over Virginia, and some from out of state, driving Chevrolets, Buicks, Cadillacs, Fords, Pontiacs, and Plymouths, dropped off 328 young men in front of the barracks at the Virginia Military Institute, near a statue of Confederate General Thomas "Stonewall" Jackson. Some forty new cadets, who had signed up to play football, arrived two weeks earlier. My high school friend and future husband was one of them. Four years later, out of the 368 new cadets, 215 graduated. All 368 young men, including those who did not graduate, are forever known as the VMI Class of 1968.

Most of the new cadets enrolling in 1964 had no idea what they were getting into. Creigh Kelley, Class of '68, described his first day and week at VMI:

Unlike most other new cadets, my grandmother, who lived about two-and-a-half hours away from VMI, dropped me off at VMI. My mother had grown up in Virginia, but I had been raised in Connecticut. My parents sent me by plane to Virginia so my grandmother could get me to VMI. My mother is the reason I ended up at VMI—she wanted me to go to a college in Virginia, and she thought VMI would be the right place. I arrived with either a footlocker or suitcase, I can't remember. I was directed, along with a sea of other young men, to what I remember to be a gymnasium, perhaps Cocke Hall, where someone paperclipped a three-by-five-inch notecard with my name and hometown and state onto the front of my shirt. That meant everyone there immediately knew my name and that I was a Yankee.

Being a Yankee was the beginning of my hell in a college soaked in Southern culture. We were sent to desks in the gym according to our selected majors and given information. I got my room assignment and maybe a class schedule. We were given a Rat Bible, a pocket-size brochure containing the history of VMI, all rules and regulations and details of the Honor System, and told we had to memorize it by the next morning. I was directed out of the gym and through the Jackson Arch (entrance to the Old Barracks) to find my room, and that is where light turned to dark. Immediately, I was being yelled at by at least thirty upperclassmen cadets on how to stand, how to say sir, and demeaned for being a Yankee. It was brutal. I later learned that these mean and aggressive young men were called the "cadre," a group of gung-ho cadets who volunteered to harass the incoming freshmen. While we freshmen had arrived a week before other upperclassmen in order to be schooled in military life, these cadre men had also arrived a week early to do that "schooling." Within seconds, I learned to "strain," with shoulders back, spine straight, and chin tucked. I learned not to speak unless spoken to, and always to say "sir" when answering. If we answered wrongly, that is, not saying sir, or saying too much, or just not the right answer, we were ordered to do an insane number of push-ups. I remember many of my new classmates breaking into tears, saying they wanted to go home.

Through the shouting, they organized us into companies by height—A through F and Band Company. I was assigned to C company. Then they marched us down to the laundry, where we were given gray fatigues, military boots, and hats. The fatigues were an awful color, and we all looked like criminals. Laundry workers measured us for our uniforms, which included a summer uniform of white pants and shirt, a winter uniform of gray wool pants and blouse, and a dress uniform comprised of a more formal blouse with gold braid and brass buttons and a large wool cape lined in red. Next, they took us to the barbershop, where they shaved our heads, which I soon learned was the first of many VMI rituals intended to cut everyone down to a common size. They returned us to the barracks, where we found our rooms on the fourth stoop, three to five men to a room. Inside, each of us was assigned a "hay" (wooden cot and cotton mattress), a desk, and a chair. By this time, most of us wanted to split, to go home, and it was probably only about 4 in the afternoon.

A little before 6 p.m., an announcement came over a loudspeaker that we were to form up in front of the barracks to prepare our march to dinner. The cadre shouted at us to strain. We heard the bugle call as the American flag flying in front of the Old Barracks was lowered. We heard the firing of the cannon, a boom that rang through the town. Then they, the cadre, marched us by company to the dining hall, Crozet Hall. Here, we learned to walk the Rat Line, which meant walking while straining and making turns at ninety-degree angles. In the dining hall, we had to walk double-time to our tables, where food was served family style in large bowls. Reaching our tables, we had to sit on the front three inches of the chair, keep our eyes straight ahead, feet flat on the floor, strain with shoulders back and chin tucked, and eat a "square meal" by raising our forks straight up from our plates and then making a right angle to our mouths, and never say a word.

We received military indoctrination for one week before our classes started. The harassment continued all week—it was hell. I cried into my pillow every night. Honestly, I just wanted to go home.

The freshmen football players who had arrived on post two weeks earlier, along with upperclassmen football players, had less of a shock. Paul Hebert, one of those freshmen, explains:

> We had to arrive early to get in shape because the first football game would occur soon after the start of the academic year. By the end of our first two weeks, we football team freshmen were already "in the know" about much of VMI, unlike most of my classmates, because we had been assigned our "dykes," senior cadet football players who were also early arrivals, and those dykes had clued us into what to expect at VMI. Every freshman gets a dyke who helps us get oriented to the military system and serves as our protectors. We had been wearing civilian clothes those two weeks before all the others arrived and had already experienced living in the barracks. But when it came to uniform measuring and head-shaving, we were thrown in with the rest of the new cadets.

The word dyke originates from the expression, "dyked-out," meaning someone is fully dressed in a formal uniform, with two white bands crisscrossed over the chest. All incoming freshmen, rats, are assigned a dyke. The role of the incoming freshman is to help his dyke get "dyked-out." The rat is to polish his shoes, clean his room, and generally take care of his dyke. The dyke is supposed to advise the freshman cadet and protect him from some of the harassment that would continue until the "breakout" from the Rat Line sometime in February or March. (The date was always a secret until the day before.) The dyke room would also serve as a refuge, as it was the only other room in the entire barracks that the rat could visit. Dykes and their roommates were relaxed and fun to be with—a relief rats often needed.

"Because of all we went through that first week at VMI, because of all the shared suffering, we rats bonded as a class. We became a brotherhood, and that is why we call each other Brother Rats," Creigh concluded.

John VanLandingham, also Class of '68, has two favorite stories about VMI. The first story is about a professor, Doc Carroll, whom John described as "pretty much a one-man premed program," who had two sayings: "VMI is not what it used to be. And never was," and "VMI separates the men from the boys; the men leave." This reflected, John said, "that many of us wanted to leave, all four years, but didn't have the courage to disappoint our parents." John had a classmate, Ron Cowardin, who, during his first weeks at VMI, used to call his mother every night and beg for permission to leave. "Even when Ron was a 2nd Class cadet (third year), Cadet Lewis White would tease Ron by suggesting that they leave at 2 a.m. Ron would get up and dressed, but Lewis would never show up."

John's second favorite story happened nearly two decades later, in 1997, when the lawsuit to admit women to VMI was coming before the Supreme Court. A friend called John to alert him to an interview at VMI by a national news program. John described the moment:

> The administration had offered up a blue-eyed, ramrod-

straight rat, who answered every question with a "yes ma'am" or "no ma'am." You could tell the reporter was getting frustrated over not getting anything newsworthy, and in desperation, she cut to the chase and asked him whether he thought women should go to VMI. He froze, apparently not having been prepped for that question, and then blurted out, "Ma'am, I don't think anyone should go to VMI."

"I always thought that was how everyone felt," John said, "a great place to be from but a miserable experience while you are there."

AN OVERVIEW OF THE CLASS OF '68

Historically, VMI has drawn most of its students from the state of Virginia. That was still true in 1968, as 62 percent of the survey respondents had graduated from a high school in Virginia. Of those who came from outside Virginia, 25 percent came from Northern states, 7 percent came from states south of Virginia, 6 percent were from western states, and three cadets came from abroad—an American from Germany, a student from Singapore, and one from Thailand. The Virginia brother rats in the class would have gone to four years of high school with no Black classmates, even though they matriculated at VMI ten years after the 1954 US Supreme Court decision, Brown vs. Board of Education, outlawing school segregation.

The strongest reason for choosing VMI was family influence—carrying on a family military tradition—reported by fifty-one men. Thirty-three said they came for the academic offerings. Twenty-two came because they got a scholarship, and of those, thirteen were recruited to play sports. Twenty-six men said they came because someone outside of the family recommended VMI to them. Although nearly half said they attended VMI because of family influence and tradition, only 10 percent had children who attended VMI.

Three-quarters of men majored in three areas: sciences (27 percent), engineering (23 percent), and history (32 percent). The remainder majored in economics (6 percent), English (7 percent), math (4 percent), and modern languages (1 percent).[6] Over 80 percent went on to postgraduate education. Thirty-three earned a master of arts or science. Twenty-six earned a master of business administration. Another thirty men earned master's degrees in a wide range of fields, such as forestry, music, and administration. Fifteen acquired law degrees, and eleven earned a doctorate in their field. Eight members of the Class of 1968 went on to become doctors and dentists. If these responses are somewhat representative of the entire class, then this is a very accomplished group of men.

Some men in the Class of '68 described their four years at VMI as living in a bubble, largely cut off from how life is lived in the rest of the town, in our families, and communities. There was not much diversity. The class had one cadet from Singapore and one from Thailand. One graduate said, "We didn't see that we had no Black cadets. I guess we had on blinders."

DIVISIONS WITHIN THE CLASS OF '68

Upon entry at VMI, the Class of '68 almost immediately divided itself into those involved in athletic teams—swimming, track, football, basketball, baseball—and those not involved in athletic teams. Paul said that while a cadet's sport was active, the cadet athlete received exemptions, called "permits," from certain military activities like marching and participating in parades. Athletes were also excused from military duty every weekday afternoon (4 to 6 p.m.), as that was when the teams practiced. In the dining hall, the "mess," athletes sat at special training tables where, as rats, they did not have to "eat a square meal" and received more and better food delivered to their table. (There was no cafeteria line at that time.) On Sundays, the day after an athletic event, athletes could sleep in while other cadets had to rise at 6:50 a.m. Of course, athletes traveled off-post for competitions and thereby were excused from classes and other duties while on these trips. Even though team athletes had to make up work from all classes missed, there was still a certain resentment or jealousy among some of the rest of the class for what seemed like extravagant privileges given to athletes. On the other hand, there was great pride throughout the corps for their teams and appreciation for athletes.

Athletes often felt that they made a lot of sacrifices of time and energy to be on an athletic team. They had to practice two to three hours every day during athletic seasons and simply could not have done the full military regimen expected of other cadets.

The class was also divided by military rank and general interest in the military. While cadets were expected to rise in military rank with each passing school year, many from the Class of '68 preferred to remain privates throughout their four years. Paul Hebert, who graduated a private, said he preferred to concentrate on athletics and academics. Another, who graduated a private, said that he was also focused on his sport and academics. A total of seventy-two graduates held military rank above private, 25 percent of the class.

NO VALEDICTORIAN

The Class of '68 graduated on June 9, 1968, and may be the only VMI class that did not have a valedictorian. The 1st Class cadets elect their valedictorian, which is not tied to academic performance but rather to respect. Late in the second semester before graduation, the class elected George Squires. John VanLandingham came in second. They respected George not only for his top grades but even more for his brave leadership as editor of *The V.M.I. Cadet* newspaper. They respected John for his leadership as president of the Honor Court.

Both Paul Hebert and I knew George Squires in high school, where he excelled academically. He was in the George Wythe High School Cadet Corps, graduating as a lieutenant.

George continued to be an excellent student at VMI and was named *Who's Who Among Students in American Universities and Colleges*. First in his class academically, it was expected that George would receive the Jackson-Hope Medal‡‡ for academic excellence. But second semester, things began to go awry for George.

As editor of *The V.M.I. Cadet* newspaper, George began expressing his displeasure with the Vietnam War and military life through anti-war editorials. And he began receiving an excessive number of demerits. In an email to John VanLandingham in 2002, George wrote,

> In addition to my own reckless, rebellious, and dumb behavior, part of the excess demerit problem was due to being boned for 'undesirable conduct' because one of our rat delivery guys didn't get the school newspaper to the Military Science Dept. on time. Gee, I wonder if the anti-war editorials had anything to do with that penalty? Irv Grodsky, the newspaper's business manager, tried to take the rap for me, but they wouldn't let him.[7]

George also went on to explain that he had received quite a few demerits from Major Halliburton, a TAC officer, following a cartoon of Halliburton drawn by fellow cadet Roddy Delk (now Judge Delk of Virginia's 5th Judicial District) that had appeared in *The V.M.I. Cadet* and depicted him as "Generalissimo Halliburtoni." That was probably not a smart thing to do, given VMI's military discipline

---

‡‡ Jackson-Hope Medals. "In 1867 the Honorable A. J. B. Beresford Hope, member of the British Parliament and representative of an association that had presented to the Commonwealth of Virginia a statue of Thomas J. Jackson, sent to Governor James L. Kemper the remainder of the statue fund, requesting that it be used for a further memorial to the great Confederate soldier. The Governor proposed and the Board of Visitors approved the establishment of two 'Jackson-Hope Medals' to be presented annually to the two most distinguished graduates of the Institute, and since the first awards in 1877, the Jackson-Hope Medals have been VMI's highest awards for scholastic achievement" (catalog. vmi.edu, Prizes, Metals and Awards).

structure. Halliburton reported to the commandant that George had disobeyed an order. George said he never heard the order. Then, soon after, the corps held a mess hall/barracks riot directed at Halliburton in support of George—beating on tables in the mess hall, beating on railings in the barracks, and shouting obscenities. Halliburton accused George of instigating it. George received more demerits. Finally, during final exams weekend, someone ransacked Halliburton's office, and again, George was accused. George denied all these charges.

Despite George never being convicted of any of these offenses against Major Halliburton, the TAC officer managed to give George enough demerits that he was denied graduation in June. Nine days before graduation, George was suspended and returned home to Richmond.

So, the Class of '68 had no valedictorian at graduation. The runner-up was John VanLandingham. The administration interviewed John about possibly taking that role and asked him what he might say. Evidently, John's reply was unsatisfactory for whatever reason, and the class had no valedictorian. The Jackson-Hope Medal went to Skip Roberts, who had the next highest grade point average.

VMI allowed George to return in the summer to take his final exams and graduate. After graduating that summer, George returned to his family home in Richmond. He worked with John VanLandingham on a Virginia Association of Student Governments (VASG) project. Yet the suspicion did not abate. That summer, Superintendent Shell asked George to meet him in a hotel in Richmond. He tried to get George to confess to the office break-in by telling him that they had his fingerprints from the office. George replied, "No sir, you don't. I've never been in that office." Later that week, a state highway patrol vehicle pulled up to his parent's home in Richmond, upsetting his parents, and took him to headquarters to be fingerprinted. He said he never heard anything again from the Institute regarding this matter.

This harsh sentence on George, one of VMI's academic stars, no doubt had a traumatic impact on him. Following VMI, George attended Duke University on an academic scholarship in a graduate history program but dropped out during the first year. After serving in the army from 1969 to 1972, George tried various trades, including bus driver and wildlife biologist, but could not settle on one. In 1975, he joined a new-age religious movement that, in George's words, "appealed to people's deepest spiritual idealism." Ten years later, he earned a degree in chiropractic medicine, met his future wife, and continued working for the church for a total of twenty-four years. But he said the church changed and became a "difficult, even destructive experience." He wrote, in his email to John, "It was as if I'd volunteered to be a character in some cosmic spiritual psychodrama and couldn't get out until it ran its course. I would end up thoroughly spent, used up, confused, drained, dazed, and disillusioned." George also had five car accidents that left him "too beat-up, burnt out, and exhausted to continue." He stopped working as a chiropractor and took a simple part-time job to recuperate.[8]

So, what impact did the rigor of VMI life—with its demanding military, physical, and academic environment and strict adherence to the Honor Code—have on other members of the Class of '68 after graduation and their moving on to what cadets often referred to as the "real world"? The one theme that does come through is a strong appreciation of the Honor Code in their lives. The Honor Code is enforced through VMI's Honor Court system. John VanLandingham was president of the Honor Court during his first-class year. His personal story touches on the responsibility he bore.

JOHN VANLANDINGHAM

★ ★ ★

CLASS OF '68,
PRESIDENT OF THE HONOR COURT

John VanLandingham said he was raised to go to VMI. John's father was a VMI graduate—Class of '43, regimental commander, first captain, electrical engineering major, and recipient of the prestigious Jackson-Hope Medal for academic excellence. His father had chosen VMI because his best friend had an older brother there who was regimental commander in 1939-40 and whose photo in full-dress uniform was on the cover of *The Saturday Evening Post* (November 11, 1939).[9] John's parents often took him and his two younger brothers to VMI, especially on football game weekends. It was a foregone conclusion that John would attend VMI, and thus, it was the only college he applied for.

Born and raised in Petersburg, Virginia, John's childhood was typical of a Southern White upbringing. Both of his parents had grown up in Petersburg. Petersburg in the 1960s was still segregated by race.

The only Black folks he knew were his mother's and grandmother's maids and cooks, caddies at the country club, and summertime truck farmers who sold on the side of the road—even though Petersburg was 50 percent Black, and the local Black college, Virginia State College (now University), brought in a lot of Black professionals. There were three high schools—one for Whites, one for Blacks, and one run by the Catholic Church. Petersburg public schools began to integrate by admitting just a few Black students in the fall of 1963 but did not fully integrate until 1970.

"Everything in our town was segregated," John told me, "including the public library where I spent many hours browsing the bookshelves in a wonderful old house. The 'Black library' was a small space in the basement. My church was segregated, and when a new, younger minister advocated for integration in his sermons, the vestry of my church fired him."

Being near Richmond, the capital of the Confederacy, Petersburg was soaked in Confederate symbols and lore. John was raised to revere the South and its leaders:

> My parents had, in the entry to their home, a famous photo of Robert E. Lee, taken astride Traveler (his horse) after the war. You could tell that because the insignia were stripped off his uniform, one of Grant's few requirements for Lee's surrender. As a young person, I read extensively about the South's Civil War effort. Petersburg was full of Civil War sites. During the year-long siege of Petersburg, Lee worshipped at my family's church in the pew just in front of my family's pew. There are still cannonballs lodged in the church walls. I was proud to be a Southerner, and I admired leaders like Stonewall Jackson. I didn't think about how that would be demeaning to Blacks, nor how those statues of Civil War generals were meant to suppress Blacks.

At home, John's parents conveyed suspicion of Blacks and Jews. For example, his parents thought Martin Luther King was a communist since J. Edgar Hoover (director of the Federal Bureau of Investigation from 1924 to 1972) said as much. His mother insinuated that she did not like Jews.

Despite an upbringing that might have resulted in John being racially or ethnically prejudiced, John broke the mold. He was politically aware in high school and widely read. He spent evenings with his best friend, Carl Tobias (now a law professor in Richmond who frequently writes for newspapers), pouring over newspapers, like the *Richmond Times Dispatch* and the *Petersburg Progress-Index*, and discussing politics—state and national. He subscribed to *Mad Magazine* and *Punch Magazine* (a British humor magazine). In high school, John read *Black Like Me* by John Howard Griffin (1961), which greatly influenced him about the harms of segregation. At graduation from high school, Carl gave him a copy of Jean-Paul Sartre's *Being and Nothingness* (1956). This book continued to peel the scales off John's eyes, inviting him to open his mind and look at the world in a new way. "My parents made us attend church every Sunday, and I sat through a lot of sermons contemplating racial inequality and hypocrisy," John said. John also had another best friend named Rosemarie Russi, a Jew. Rosemarie's parents had fled Poland just ahead of Hitler. Her mother had studied painting under the famous German American painter Hans Hoffman (1880-1966), one of the most important characters of postwar American art. He and Carl considered the Russi house akin to an art museum.

AT VMI

By the time John matriculated at VMI, many of his foundational values were already formed, and they were, by Southern standards, liberal and a bit anti-VMI. On the other hand, he didn't talk politics with too many classmates. John was on the swim team and devoted most of his time to his studies, sports, and keeping his head down to avoid getting demerits. Since he was on the swim team, he escaped much of the Rat Line from October to the end of March during his first year, which meant not having to strain at meals or partake in military duty in the afternoons. His main buddies were on the swim team from all four classes.

And John had a lot of other activities. He was chair of the ring committee (to design the class ring) as a 3rd Class cadet, then served on the Honor Court as a 2nd and 1st Class cadet. Throughout his time at VMI, John kept up with the news and did not feel he was living in a bubble. But he said he felt lonely at VMI. He did not drink alcohol, so he did not attend back rooms of Lexington bars, where cadets hid out and drank on Wednesday afternoons and Saturday nights.

John dreaded returning to VMI after Christmas and spring breaks. "I can remember clearly, still, the feeling of dread when my parents would drive me back to barracks after a Christmas or spring or summer break, cresting the last hill into Lexington and praying that the barracks would miraculously be gone." Other graduates from other classes told him they had the same feelings.

Throughout his years at VMI, John became increasingly interested in race relations, questioning the status quo while following events of the Civil Rights Movement. The summer after his third class year (1966), he attended a speech by Dr. Martin Luther King Jr. at Virginia State College, the all-Black college in Petersburg. He remembered that there were exactly four White people in a crowd of about five thousand—his liberal Catholic neighbors, the Colemans, himself, and his date, a Jewish girl.

During John's 1st Class year (1967-68), he served as president of the VMI Honor Court. He also joined a statewide group called the Virginia Association of Student Governments and served as chair of their Honor Code committee. In the spring of 1968, there was a meeting in Roanoke for all the members to elect new leaders. As John was graduating and leaving his position, he brought with him to this meeting a 2nd Class cadet. The members were to vote on the next president of the VASG. Of the two candidates, both from other colleges, one was White and the other was Black. John thought both were qualified, but he voted for the Black student because he felt it would be important to have some diversity in leadership. His fellow cadet was shocked.

The point, John told me, is that he was all for civil rights.

John said he didn't talk much about his feelings and opinions concerning American race relations or the Civil Rights Movement with his fellow cadets. He remembers watching a classmate, now a minister, dance on a tabletop when Martin Luther King was assassinated and decided it was best to keep his opinions to himself. But he had a few friends with whom he discussed ideas. One was George Squires and his close cadet buddies Bill Boyer, Ron Cowardin, and Lewis White, whose girlfriend and later wife was vehemently anti-war. George had ruffled a few feathers when, as editor of *The V.M.I. Cadet*, he printed a banner headline in the spring of 1968 that read, "Otis died for your sins." Otis Redding, arguably one of the greatest American singers of soul and rhythm and blues, a Black man, died in December 1967 in a plane crash in Wisconsin at twenty-six. To compare him to Jesus, as having died for our sins, was stretching the envelope on what ideas would be tolerable at VMI.

I asked John whether his professors or classmates at VMI ever discussed current events in or outside of classes, as many of his classmates said they were living in a bubble, not paying much attention to what else was happening or having much access to TV, radio, or newspapers. John said that only his psychology professor, Dean Foster, did. Once, he required his class to attend a lecture at Washington and Lee University by a writer who had graduated from W&L. The writer was Tom Wolfe, whose writing John did not know. Wolfe told stories for two hours about novelist Ken Kesey and his Merry Pranksters, which became his book, *The Electric Kool-Aid Acid Test*. When it came out in October 1968, he bought and devoured it. The book chronicled the very opposite of VMI life or growing up in Petersburg, Virginia.

It's a story of how Kesey, in the 1960s, led a group of psychedelic sympathizers around the country in a painted bus, experimenting with LSD-induced "acid tests" along the way. It is considered one of the greatest books about the history of American hippies.

A current event that should have caught the attention of John, the cadets, and the professors at VMI was the 1965 murder of Jonathan Daniels in Alabama. He was shot for helping Blacks register to vote. Despite this happening in John's first year at VMI, he said he didn't remember learning about Daniel's murder while there.

Even though John kept his head down and opinions to himself, he suspected that the administration knew his liberal anti-VMI views, which, he believes, resulted in his class having no valedictorian. When the administration suspended George for excess demerits two weeks before graduation, it seemed that John would take his place. Colonel Dillard, who advised valedictorians on their speeches, asked John to meet with him. "It was a good chat," John remembers, "but I never heard more. Our class did not have a valedictorian. I have always assumed the administration feared what I might say about the war in Vietnam or the administration."

AFTER VMI

The summer after his graduation, John worked for the VASG to prepare a program for Virginia public schools to encourage kids to go to college. At that time, Virginia had a low college attendance rate. He got George Squires to work with him. He also worked with two students from William and Mary. He and George, ever the jokesters, would send postcards to their VMI Brother Rat Bill Boyer, pretending to be from George Wallace (1919-1998), the notorious governor of Alabama who was a vocal and stanch segregationist. They knew that Boyer, a liberal progressive, would find it funny.

In the fall of 1968, John entered the University of Virginia School of Law in Charlottesville. In December, he dropped out. He had been reading books about Malcolm X (1925-1965) and Eldridge

Cleaver's (1935-1998) *Soul on Ice* (1968), a collection of essays on race and Black empowerment. Both men were highly visible civil rights leaders. Malcolm X was an African American Muslim minister and a spokesman for the Nation of Islam until 1964. He advocated for Black empowerment and the promotion of Islam within the Black community. Leroy Eldridge Cleaver was a Black American writer and political activist who became an early leader of the Black Panthers. As a result, John realized he did not want to continue his current track—a law degree, marriage to his Mary Baldwin College girlfriend, returning to Petersburg, joining the country club, and playing golf. John was also questioning everything about American society, disturbed by racism and racial segregation, supportive of the Civil Rights Movement and racial justice, and trying to find his way. Where would he fit in?

After dropping out of UVA, John went through some rough moments. He had grown his hair long and had a mustache. People considered him a hippy. When he attended the graduation of the VMI Class of '69 in support of his close friend from the swim team, Lee Galloway, Lee's father refused to shake hands with him due to his appearance. In addition, John's mother told him that dropping out of law school was the biggest disappointment of his father's life. "She knew how to hurt me," he said. The summer after John left UVA, his brother Jimbo decided not to return to VMI after his rat year, and his mother said the same thing to him.

John stayed in Charlottesville for the rest of the academic year and enrolled in a graduate program in education, joining his friend and Brother Rat Ron Cowardin. John remembers that he and Ron had one class with two young professors fresh from their doctorates. They spent their weekly classes talking about books, such as Herbert Marcuse's *One-Dimensional Man: Studies in the Ideology of Advanced Industrial Society* (1964). Marcuse argued that the modern "affluent" society represses even those who are successful within it while maintaining their complacency through the satisfaction of consumer culture. The book is a wide-ranging critique of contemporary capitalism and the Communist society of the Soviet Union, documenting the parallel rise of new forms of social repression in both these societies—plenty of food for thought in 1969. These young professors thought John and Ron could help them understand the life of UVA students—"when we knew nothing about typical college life because of VMI." Meanwhile, John got involved in the UVA chapter of the Students for a Democratic Society, which was organizing protests over the role of its Board of Visitors, UVA's governing body, in racial segregation. He was learning firsthand lessons about our society that would eventually lead him back to law.

While in Charlottesville, John decided to try a date-matching service, the kind where you answer questions like "Would you rather read a book or watch TV?" and it matches you up with allegedly compatible girls. The service matched him with a senior at William and Mary college in Williamsburg, Va., a Miss Dee Curwen from Fieldale, Virginia. His former VASG pals, who had attended William and Mary, knew and liked her, and so John asked her out. They dated, fell in love, and ended up living together, off and on, for seven years. Several years later, they moved to Oregon together.

John describes 1969 and 1970 as his "attempted hippy period." By the summer of 1969, John had decided not to return to UVA and returned to Petersburg to work in a cigarette factory. That did not last long. He and George Squires, who also dropped out of Duke University graduate school, traveled around the US by car, sleeping in the car and exploring. They traveled to the Rocky Mountains, Death Valley, Los Angeles, where they bought some mescaline, a psychedelic drug that occurs naturally in the San Pedro cactus, and tried it in Big Sur, California. They then headed home via Texas, where they visited their Brother Rat and good buddy Bill Boyer (who had received the fake postcards from George Wallace), who was doing his military service at Fort Hood. Boyer taught them how to smoke the marijuana they bought in San Francisco. These were heady days.

John was up for more exploration of life than his upbringing in Petersburg and four years at VMI had afforded him. He had spent the first twenty-two years of his life in Virginia, had taken a brief trip west, and now was ready for more. In September 1969, he moved to Washington, DC, to join his girlfriend, Dee, and her sister in a large rental house where young people paid rent by the bedroom. He made enough money to get by, driving a taxicab in Alexandria. He participated in anti-Vietnam War marches and volunteered for Ralph Nader in the early part of Ralph's career as a consumer advocate and environmentalist. He avoided VMI and all his brother rats—except George Squires, Bill Boyer, and Ron Cowardin.

In June 1970, John embarked on his second exploratory trip across the US with three others—his girlfriend Dee, Dee's college roommate Debbie, and Tommy, someone he met in DC. They drove Dee's father's Edsel station wagon, a nine-passenger vehicle made only from 1958 to 1960, which stands out in John's mind. (The Ford Motor Company considered it a failed product.) They backpacked into the Rockies, explored Mesa Verde, Colorado, cooled off in Las Vegas casinos, and explored San Francisco while staying in a youth hostel. When they tired of San Francisco, they decided to visit one of Dee's college friends from William & Mary, Delores, who was taking summer school classes at the University of Oregon. When they arrived, Delores's class was meeting in a nearby national forest campground with huge Douglas fir trees. A clear, cold stream ran down from the Cascade Mountains. The salmon were spawning, and the group jumped in nude. They thought they had found the best place in the world. Of the four on that trip, three settled years later in Oregon.

John, Dee, Debbie, and Tommy returned to the East Coast, and the following February, John was called to military service, which had been deferred since September 1968 when he enrolled in law school. President Nixon was winding down the Vietnam War, and the army had too many second lieutenants. So, they offered him a deal: instead of serving on active duty for two years, a VMI graduate's commitment, he could serve four months, with several years thereafter in the reserves. The downside was that he would not qualify for the GI bill that would have paid for postgraduate education, a home mortgage, or loans for a business. John happily accepted this deal and spent four months at Fort Benning, Georgia, a depressing and lonely time.

After John's stint at Fort Benning, he and Dee moved back to Eugene, Oregon, in the summer of 1971. But they could not find jobs. In the fall, it rained too much, so they gave up and took a Greyhound bus back to Virginia, over 2,600 miles away. When they arrived, they admitted that they had forgotten how much they disliked Virginia, so they headed back to Oregon again in February 1972, this time driving the Edsel. To make ends meet, John worked as a delivery boy and learned pottery and how to develop film. He fly-fished, cross-country skied, and backpacked in the Cascades. John was still unwinding from four years at VMI.

In the fall of 1973, perhaps renewed in spirit and having fulfilled his need to experience hippy life, John realized he wanted to try law school again. He applied to UVA once more and got an interview. He again took a bus across the country for that interview, but he was rejected. It came as a bit of a shock, but not to give up, he applied to the University of Oregon, was accepted, and started his law degree in August 1974. John noted that U of O was very different from UVA. "Students at Oregon wore T-shirts instead of suits, forty percent of the class was women, professors were friendly, and many of the students were five or ten years removed from college and were more mature and fun."

After graduating from law school in June 1977, John started working for Lane County Legal Aid, a publicly funded nonprofit law firm that provided free legal assistance on civil matters to low-income Oregonians. He specialized in landlord/tenant law and, later, affordable housing development. He remained there for his career. In the late 1980s, John's work began to focus on legislative advocacy with local governments and the state concerning tenant rights and affordable housing. The firm merged with Oregon Law Center in 2017, a larger and better-funded statewide legal aid program. John also served twelve years on the Eugene Planning Commission and then another twelve on the State's Land Conservation and Development Commission, seven years as the chair.

In August 1980, John married Martha Walters, one of his classmates from the University of Oregon School of Law. Dee, still a good friend, made the wedding cakes. Martha worked for a private law firm specializing in civil rights law and sex discrimination in employment. Their two children were born in 1984 and 1986. In 2006, the governor of Oregon appointed Martha to the Oregon Supreme Court, and in 2018, her Supreme Court peers chose her as the chief justice, the first woman to hold this position. She retired from that position at the end of 2022.

LOOKING BACK

Although the admission of women to VMI occurred nearly two decades after John's graduation, I asked him how he felt about that decision, as it was quite controversial at the time. John thought it was only fair that women be allowed to go to VMI. "A VMI diploma is certainly an advantage in Virginia, and it opens up a lot of doors," he said. "I never liked the Mary Baldwin College Virginia Women's Institute for Leadership program; it reminded me of the 'separate but equal' public schools during segregation. I also knew that many women could be successful in the Rat Line and meet the physical demands," he said. That those physical demands were not so binding for success at VMI, John relayed that he had a rat-year roommate who could not do a single push-up but had managed to get through VMI. He thought single-sex colleges were bad because it is "making boys act crazy when they finally had dates." John said that he had been thinking about women's admission since he entered VMI in 1964. To wit, he and his Brother Rat Ron Cowardin had written a class paper for psychology with professor Dean Foster on "VMI as a utopian society." A key part of their proposal was that women would be admitted.

I asked John if he ever thought about the Confederate statues, symbolism, and rituals on post when he was a student at VMI. He said he did not think about it until recently. "I admired Lee and Jackson, the cadets at the Battle of New Market, and the Southerners in the Civil War. I never believed that the Civil War was about states' rights. It was clearly about the South's economy, preserving all that free labor." When the Jackson statue was removed, John felt it was the right thing to do. He liked the statue, but he also understood what it represented to Black cadets, the same as the statues on Monument Avenue in Richmond. "I regret that doing so has been so divisive. During our cadetship, I attended church on Sundays at the Robert E. Lee Memorial Episcopal Church next to W&L. Several years ago, after two years of debate, the congregation removed Lee from the name, and in the process, it lost about half its members."

John was a two-year member of the VMI Honor Court, serving as president of the court in his final year. The court always consisted of four seconds and ten firsts. "I was proud of the court and proud to be its president. And I was proud of the Honor Code." John remembers two "drumming-out" ceremonies in his first class year:

> In the middle of the night, with the eerie pounding of a drum and all cadets gathered on the stoops of Old Barracks, the Court marched out into the center, and I, walking in a circle around the guard house, recited these words: "Tonight, your Honor Court has met and found [person's name] to be guilty of an Honor Code violation. He has placed personal gain above personal honor. He has left the Institute, never to return. His name shall never be mentioned again."

John recalls being so nervous that he could not stop shaking:

I realized then, and do still, that it was a barbaric thing to do. There were rumors that, in the old corps, the convicted cadet was made to walk out into the courtyard with the Honor Court. We did not do that. The convicted cadet was taken to a motel in town with one of his roommates. Barbaric but also effective.

This drumming-out ceremony is the essence of VMI's "single sanction" Honor Code. If you are convicted of an Honor Code violation—lying, stealing, cheating, or failing to report such in another cadet that you know of—you are not allowed a second chance. My wife does not believe in the single-sanction Honor Code. She thinks there should be second chances. I respect her views.

Being president of the Honor Court brought prestige as well as challenges. Cadets would ask John if it would be "all right," meaning not an Honor Code violation, to do something they wanted to do. He hated that. He felt strongly that it was their responsibility to figure that out and decide for themselves. He also presided over two acquittals.

During John's first-class year as president of the Honor Court, he wanted to write a history of the court. He got permission to skip the spring Field Training Exercises (FTX) for that week to gather information. He wrote to all past presidents but got few responses and thus did not finish that project.

I asked John how far the Honor Code extended into treating others with respect, especially those of a different race. I asked this because I have observed the hazing of rats, which is highly disrespectful of the person hazed. They are shouted at and often made to do an insane number of push-ups. I had always found those two things to be contradictory. He replied that he thought the Honor Code was effective in addressing the aspect of honor for which it was designed: a cadet shall not lie, cheat, or steal and shall not tolerate those who do. But, he said, I was asking about a different kind of honor—honoring all people and treating all with respect. "I did not view that as part of the Honor Court's mission then. I now respect that form of honor, and I hope that I live it. But I don't know how that would fit or work within the VMI Honor Code. Disrespect is more subjective than cheating on a test and likely would require something other than a single sanction."

I asked him to reflect upon the Rat Line. Did he feel that the harassment of rats was the right thing to do? I had seen how vicious it can be. It has a long tradition, from the very earliest days of VMI, but is it still appropriate in today's world? John felt I had conflated two different things. There is the Rat Line of marching in a straight line with your chin pulled in while in barracks, eating a "square meal" in the mess hall, or doing difficult physical tasks as a group. Then there is the more hidden hazing stuff, like "straining parties," where several rats are gathered and made to stand in the straining position for ten or fifteen minutes, or beatings with coat hangers, or "sweat parties," where rats are made to do many sit-ups, push-ups, and other physically demanding acts until they are in a sweat. John said he experienced very little of that as a rat. "I think because I followed the best guidance—do not stand out or get noticed." He also missed a lot of the other parts of the Rat Line by being a member of the rat swim team from October to March. "Because of that, I missed a lot of the afternoon training, and we had our swim team table in the mess hall." After his rat year, John refused to participate in harrassing rats. He feels that the Rat Line allowed power for bad people to abuse others. "Still, that happens in life generally, not just in VMI's Rat Line, so maybe that is an important thing to learn."

On the positive side, John feels that the Rat Line accomplishes the goal of building team spirit.

I asked John whether he knew VMI's history before he went and what he learned years later. Because of his father's cadetship, he knew a fair amount about VMI before attending:

I was a bit of a Civil War buff as a young person and read extensively, so I knew about Stonewall Jackson and New Market and that Robert E. Lee was buried nearby [at Washington & Lee University, next door to VMI]. I knew my way around the barracks from my trips there with my parents. At the same time, I was also reading a lot about racial discrimination and segregation in the South, and I was aware that VMI, like all public colleges in Virginia, was segregated. And I thought that was wrong.

Thinking back over his years at VMI, John has come to the following conclusions. He liked that VMI shaved everyone's heads upon matriculation. He views hair as "a definite status symbol." "The same is true for civilian clothes, cars, and drinking," he said. "I liked the idea of everyone being reduced to the same level."

Second, he liked VMI's small size and the way the class system worked, which encouraged him to get involved. "I never anticipated running for class office our rat year [he tied for all three offices—president, vice president, and historian but lost each one in separate runoff elections] or being chairman of the ring committee or being on the Honor Court or being co-captain of the swim team. I grew a lot at VMI. I think I would not have had those wonderful experiences at a larger school."

On the downside, he became aware, especially during his last year at VMI, that his political views about the Vietnam War, integration, and other issues were significantly different from most of his classmates. "And they still are," he judged. "I did not attend our five-year class reunion in 1973, I think, for that reason."

He also had a very disappointing experience right at the beginning of his first class year that he still remembers vividly and feels was wrong. At the beginning of the 1967-68 school year, in his new role as president of the Honor Court, he met with the commandant. John asked him to commit to not allowing TAC officers or administration to use the Honor Code to catch cadets breaking the rules. Using the Honor Code means forcing cadets to admit to something and then issuing demerits for the offense.

As mentioned earlier, for many decades, including the 1960s, VMI enforced through "stick checks" the rule that all cadets need to be where they are supposed to be after Taps. If a cadet is absent from his room at that time and not in an authorized place, such as the bathroom or a study hall, with approval, he is honor-bound to report himself to the commandant's office.

Reporting oneself resulted in demerits, penalty tours, or confinement to post. John explains,

> What I wanted the commandant to agree to was that he and TAC officers would not force cadets to answer questions about whether they had done something wrong. The stick-check approach was okay, but what was not okay was calling in a cadet to the commandant's office and asking where he was at a certain time. I thought the commandant agreed.

But in December 1967, when John was in the barracks study room, studying for final exams, word came that a stick check was happening. Only certain people, such as the Honor Court president, were allowed to be out of their room and stay up late, that is, past Taps, in the barracks study room. However, two other roommates were missing from their room without permission—Rev Jones and Alfred Smith—who were also studying for exams. When word came that a TAC officer was doing a stick check, they ran to a nearby bathroom, as bathrooms were always an "all right place." John continued,

> The TAC officer came into the study room and over to me and said that he had looked into my barracks room and noted that four of the beds were empty. Since John had permission to be out of his room, as did one other roommate, the TAC

officer figured that the other two were not permitted to be out and were probably hiding in the bathroom. So, he asked me where they were.

Here was the dilemma. If John answered the question, the Honor Code required that he answer it honestly. If he refused to answer, he would be punished with penalty #1, which was fifteen demerits out of sixty allowed in a semester at that time, four months of confinement, meaning unable to leave post, and sixty hours of penalty tours, marching with a rifle on Wednesday and Saturday afternoons, a cadet's usual free time. "I refused to answer the question." John clearly recalled,

> He then reported me for failure to answer an official question. He ordered me to meet with the superintendent the following morning. I expected the superintendent to honor my agreement with the commandant.§§ He did not and did not allow me to explain further, as I stood at attention in full coatee. I went home for Christmas break crushed that I had been betrayed.

John was punished with penalty #1.

I asked John about the recent changes at VMI, resulting from the internal and external reviews of racial and other controversial issues surrounding Confederate symbols and rituals. John supports these reviews:

> Unlike some of my classmates, I do not consider critical race theory to be a communist plot. I feel very positive about the future of VMI. I suspect some alums will fight like crazy to

---

§§ The commandant oversees student discipline and military training at VMI. The superintendent is the overall director of the Institute. The commandant would be equivalent to the dean of students and the superintendent as college president.

reverse these changes, but I hope that the pragmatists, like Virginia State Senate Republican Leader, our Brother Rat Tommy Norment, will win out and keep VMI on this course, which I think will make VMI a better place.

As a former Honor Court president, John wondered whether there should be any changes to the Honor System at VMI. John feels that defendants should have lawyers if they wish. There should be diversity on the court. John concluded, "I have heard that the number of Honor Code violation trials currently is far greater than in my day. That troubles me, and I would want to understand why and reduce that."

THE PRELUDE

★ ★ ★

*"The farther backward you can look,
the farther forward you are likely to see."*
—Winston Churchill

A college like VMI, called The Citadel, is in Charleston, South Carolina. Like VMI, it was first an arsenal with soldiers, built in 1822, just four years after the Lexington Arsenal was constructed. The Citadel was built in direct response to an 1822 slave rebellion (more about that later) and then converted to a military college in 1843 by the state of South Carolina. I wondered whether VMI had a similar history of being built to put down slave rebellions or whether the nationwide abolitionist movement had Virginians worried about a coming civil war, and they wanted their own defense. As it turns out, VMI has a different history to that of The Citadel.

In 1836, a group of Virginia citizens set out to create a college that would educate young men to become citizen-soldiers and leaders of the highest caliber of honesty and integrity. They would train in engineering, science, modern languages, and military art. In 1839, they opened their new college on the site of a former Virginia militia arsenal built in 1818 that held weapons from the War of 1812, guarded by soldiers, and they named it the Virginia Military Institute.

The new institute was modeled like two other famous military schools of the day—L'École Polytechnique in Palaiseau, France, near Paris, founded in 1794, and the United States Military Academy at

West Point, New York, founded in 1802. The Military Academy at West Point had also drawn much of its inspiration and formulation from the École Polytechnique.

VMI began with a foundational Honor Code that said its cadets could not lie, cheat, or steal, nor could they protect others who did so, and anyone caught violating the Honor Code, even once, would be sent home. VMI has upheld its Honor Code to this day, with an elected Honor Court made up of cadets, and has maintained its "single sanction" rule, which means there is no second chance. One lie or dishonorable act results in dismissal.

It's a nice, sweet story. Innocent. A neat package. But is it the whole story?

Most histories of VMI begin with the 1839 story. It might be one of the most well-documented college histories in the United States. A four-volume history of the Institute, by Colonel William Couper,[10] entitled *One Hundred Years at V.M.I.*, was published in 1939 in celebration of VMI's first 100 years. In 1978, Henry A. Wise, Class of '27, published *Drawing Out the Man—The VMI Story*.[11] VMI museum director and historian Colonel Keith A. Gibson published a history in 2010 entitled *Virginia Military Institute*.[12] Danny Hogan, in 2019, published *Historical Infrastructure of the Virginia Military Institute and Related Biographies*, inspired by his 2015 class reunion.[13] And in 2020, Jonson Miller published *Engineering Manhood: Race and the Antebellum Virginia Military Institute*.[14] In addition to these detailed histories are biographies of some of VMI's founders, like Claudius Crozet[15] and John Thomas Lewis Preston.[16] VMI also has volumes of archival materials dating back to the founding of the Institute in 1839. These histories begin with the conversion of the Lexington Arsenal into a military institute and describe in detail what VMI was like through the decades, who taught there, and the origins of traditions.

I decided to take a step back, explore VMI's history from a larger societal context, and answer the questions that had swirled around in my head for decades. We have seen VMI's strict military style while being an excellent academic institution. Why was all this created? I wanted to know why the faculty and students, from the start and up to today, are honorary members of the Virginia militia, a military force from the earliest colonial times. I wanted to know whether fear of slave rebellions or a coming civil war over abolition might have had anything to do with the founding of VMI. I wanted to know to what extent the Virginia plantation aristocrats supported the founding and continued success of VMI and why? I wanted to know why the legislature of the Commonwealth of Virginia supported the founding of VMI and what they expected VMI to do for the state of Virginia. Why was VMI created in the late 1830s, when Congress had already established the United States Military Academy in West Point, New York, better known as "West Point"? Were they not duplicating efforts? Why did the state of Virginia want to have its own military college? Virginian young men were already attending West Point.

What inspired the creation of VMI? How would it be different from West Point? Or why would a duplicative effort be needed at all? There was already a men's college in Lexington, Washington College (later named Washington and Lee), so why build a second men's college right next door?

The USA was still a new country when VMI was conceived, a mere sixty years after the declaration of independence from Britain. The opening of VMI in 1839 sits twenty-seven years after the War of 1812 with the British and twenty-two years before the US Civil War. I wondered whether that had any significance. We were a new nation, still struggling to fend off the British, who still wanted to defeat us, and we had plenty of internal struggles over slavery. How did VMI fit into this picture, if at all? And why was George Washington so revered at VMI? Of course, he was our first president. But was there something else, some other connection to VMI?

Then, I wanted to know how VMI cadets were drawn into fighting the Battle of New Market and why the Institute was burned in retaliation. Why did VMI hang onto Confederate symbols? I felt the answers would help me understand how VMI shaped cadets through the decades and the Class of '68.

While all the published histories of VMI provide insights, Jonson Miller's history of VMI, from its founding to the Battle of New Market, provided some of the best answers to my flurry of questions.

Influenced by Jonson Miller and my own research, I concluded that there were at least four main drivers behind the formation of VMI, and all of these drivers reach back in time to the earliest history of Virginia and the wealthier English settlers: 1) a means to strengthen the Virginia militia, 2) a continuing fear of slave uprisings, 3) Western Virginia's quest for political influence through acquiring the right of all White men to vote, and 4) the need for transportation engineers in Virginia.

So, let's go back to before VMI was formed to see how each of these factors played a part.

A BRIEF HISTORY OF VIRGINIA

The original Virginia plantations were built by the younger sons of English small and large landowners, men who could not inherit land in England due to the rule of primogeniture, inheritance of property by the eldest son only. The Virginia Company offered them the opportunity to own land and grow profitable crops rather than become priests or merchants. At the time, land ownership signified class status. The more land owned, the greater the status, respect, and political power. Getting their hands on large plots of land was every Englishman's greatest aspiration. The male English immigrants envisaged themselves becoming landed gentry in America. Back in England, many of these immigrant second and third sons had served under King Charles I and thus were called the "cavaliers."¶¶ These earliest male settlers also brought their own portions of family wealth to Virginia, at times moving entire homes made of brick from

---

¶¶ The word "cavaliers" is still with us. Cavaliers is the nickname for sports teams today at the University of Virginia.

England and transporting fine English furnishings.

The Virginia Company, and later the English kings James I and Charles I, realized that the only way to make the Virginia colony economically successful was to grow tobacco, as there was no gold to be found. The Virginia Company had preferred that the colonists develop a mixed economy, and various industries had been tried, such as silk-making and ironworks. Colonists grew corn and wheat for their own consumption, but tobacco became the only successful export crop. John Rolfe (1585-1622) imported the first tobacco seeds to Virginia's colonists from an island outside the continent, probably Trinidad. He shared them with other colonial farmers to experiment with tobacco growing to establish a profitable industry that would compete with the already successful enterprise of the Spanish. Spanish tobacco was popular in England and throughout Europe and very profitable to planters.

At the time Virginia was colonized, England was a feudal manorial society "where economic, political, and social affairs were run by and for landed aristocrats."[17] This was the social system that the English brought to Virginia and other states, especially Southern states. While estates in England were annually productive, with mixed crops and animals, and did not need to be continually expanded, in Virginia, tobacco farming required large amounts of land because the plant used up key nutrients in the soil, particularly nitrogen, in just two to three years. Farmers had to clear and plant new fields regularly, so growing tobacco required owning large tracts of land. That meant ever-growing numbers of laborers to plant and harvest the tobacco. To be successful, a tobacco planter needed to continue acquiring land and cheap labor. As Colin Woodward explains in his book *American Character*:

> These self-identified 'Cavaliers' largely succeeded in . . . turning the lowland of Virginia, Maryland, southern Delaware, and northeastern North Carolina into a country gentleman's

paradise. They had indentured servants and, later, slaves taking the role of the peasantry. Based on English values, Tidewater plantation owners placed a high value 'on respect for authority and tradition and very little on equality or public participation in politics.'[18]

We will see how important this low value on equality or public participation in politics influenced the formation of VMI.

Virginia Tidewater tobacco planters had about two centuries of financial success—indeed, large accumulations of wealth—until things began to fall apart. By the early 1830s, tobacco had depleted much of Virginia's agricultural land of nutrients. Planters either had to expand into new territory or find another crop. But what would grow on nutrient-poor land?

Planters had always sold slaves in times of income need, but now they increasingly depended upon selling slave children and adults further south to make ends meet. At the same time, there was a growing movement to abolish slavery in both the North and South. The wealthy Tidewater plantation owners felt extremely threatened. If they could not expand their territory and slavery was abolished, they were doomed. Wealthy plantations began to lose money, and many went into serious debt, trying to maintain their former high lifestyle. Their way of life seemed to be slipping away. The only apparent way to retain it was to hold onto slavery and expand their holdings westward toward the Kansas and Nebraska territories and south into Central and South America. Southern states openly explored acquiring Mexico and Brazil to create new plantations and expand slavery.

In the early 1800s, when the formation of VMI was being considered, the aristocrats of the day included many familiar names, such as George Washington, Thomas Jefferson, James Madison, Edmund Ruffin, the Randolph family, the Wise family, and the Cocke family. These families strategically intermarried to prevent their holdings from fragmenting and combined plantations when possible. As we shall see, some of these families were intimately involved in the formation and continued support of VMI.

Virginia planters had all the political power in the state. Southern planters controlled state governments, as only men with substantial landholdings could vote. Therefore, one might conclude that these planters wanted their states to have their own militaries—loyal to the state rather than the Union. Thus, they may have had a direct interest in supporting the development and sustenance of VMI. It appears they wanted a military college to create citizen-soldiers and officers who would strengthen the existing Virginia militia to put down potential slave uprisings and defend the state from the growing threat of a civil war. They wanted to develop more transportation engineers to grow railroads and canals for the transport of crops.

And so we return to our list of four drivers.

THE VIRGINIA MILITIA

The first factor that appears to have influenced the formation of VMI was a need to produce offers for the Virginia militia. The Virginia militia had existed in the state from the earliest colonial times to protect colonial settlers from Native American raids that naturally occurred as English settlers increasingly took Native American land. The various county-level militias helped settlers expand further into Native American territories by pushing them off their land.

Militias were composed of White men from all classes of society, with the poor and landless being the most numerous, and their officers came from the most prominent planter families. Officers of the Virginia militia did not have the same rank or prestige as British officers and were paid much less. Counties formed regiments in response to threats or attacks, as needed, and every man between the ages of eighteen and sixty was expected to know how to use a musket and respond to calls to serve. It does not appear that there were well-trained units, or even well-armed units, until about the mid-1700s, when French expansion into the Ohio Valley became a serious threat to westward English expansion. Here, we see the influence of George Washington, whipping into shape the Virginia militia.

During 1753-54, George Washington, twenty-one, inherited a large plantation on the Potomac River named Mount Vernon. He had served as an aide-de-camp to British Major General Braddock and his 3,000 British soldiers in a war against the French in the Ohio Valley. The purpose of the campaign was to throw out a French army that was establishing forts in the Ohio Valley and make peace with Native American tribes in the same territory.

Even though the campaign was a failure and Braddock died from wounds, Washington's volunteer service to the cause was revered by then Virginia Governor Dinwiddie, who had strong economic interests in the Ohio Valley through the Ohio Company. Washington had learned a great deal about leading soldiers and warfare strategy from his experience in this campaign and was highly regarded by soldiers and the governor for the role he played despite the defeat. In 1755, Governor Dinwiddie decided to form a statewide Virginia militia to continue the campaign against the French and put it under the leadership of George Washington, now twenty-three. Dinwiddie not only put Washington in charge of the Virginia Regiment "but the supreme commander of all military forces in Virginia."[19] While Washington was chafed at the lower rank and pay compared to British officers, he took the post anyway because he aspired to a British military career. [20,21]

Washington served as Virginia Regiment commander for five years. He resigned on December 31, 1758, to return to his home in Mount Vernon, restore his health, and marry Mary Dandridge Custis.[22]

Washington is credited with being the first commander of the Virginia troops to bring order, discipline, and professionalism to the corps. At the end of his service, "twenty-seven officers from the Virginia Regiment banded together to laud Washington in a farewell message."[23] They wrote that his resignation is "disagreeable news" and that "the happiness we have enjoy'd and the Honor we have acquir'd . . . have implanted so sensible an Affection in the Minds of us all, that we cannot be silent at this critical Occasion. In our earliest Infancy you took us under your Tuition, train'd us up in the Practice of that Discipline which alone can constitute good Troops, from punctual Observance of which you never suffer'd the least Deviation."

The letter continues for several more paragraphs of similar accolades.[24]

While information is sketchy, it appears that the Virginia Regiment was disbanded and reinstituted several times in the following two decades to fight various wars with Native Americans under a succession of leaders. In 1775, the Virginia Regiment was again formed to fight in the Revolutionary War, with George Washington as commander, and continued its presence as a fighting force up through the Civil War.

Between the Revolutionary War and the Civil War, many states, especially Southern states, saw themselves as independent units that needed to govern and protect themselves. Because each state had been founded by different cultural or religious groups or capitalist enterprises, the new USA was not one cohesive culture.[25] The union of states was still new and fragile. A Northern movement to abolish slavery gained ground during this period, and abolitionists pressured all states to outlaw slavery. Southern states, unlike the more industrial North, depended on slavery to operate their large agricultural economies. Believing that the North was threatening their economic and social way of life, which included much leisure time for the elite plantation families, the South clamored for less federal government and more self-determination. Culturally, the North and South were growing apart, with slavery decreasing in the North and increasing in the South.

In 1794, with Eli Whitney's patent of the cotton gin—a machine for separating the seeds out of cotton, allowing the fiber to be worked into fabrics—the demand for slaves to plant and pick cotton increased. Southern plantation owners became even more economically dependent on slavery just as sentiment against it was rising in both the North and South. While Virginia did not grow cotton, it stood with the other Southern states. Together, they could not imagine a Southern economy without slavery, and they argued that each state should have the right to make its own laws regarding slavery.

The North had a population of 20 million, mostly White people; the South had about 5 million White people and 4 million enslaved people (of mostly African origin). Other cultural differences between North and South were found in food, customs, English accents, and religion. Southerners called all Northerners "Yankees," a derisive term originally used by the English in the first century of colonialism to refer to the Dutch, but the term grew to mean all New Englanders.

Yet certain forces helped to keep the states united. Both Northern and Southern aristocracy valued education and sent their children for a university education. The oldest universities in the thirteen colonies were in Massachusetts (Harvard University, 1636), Virginia (The College of William and Mary, 1693), Connecticut (Yale University, 1701), and Pennsylvania (University of Pennsylvania, 1740). Wealthy landowners in the South regularly sent their sons to study at universities in the North, such as Harvard and Yale, and, later, after independence, to the US Military Academy at West Point, New York.

President Thomas Jefferson founded the federal military academy at West Point, New York, to create a military that was representative of all the states. The nation was young, only about twenty-six years old. It not only needed a military to protect it, but it also needed help holding it together—to have one military culture. Jefferson believed that students should come from all sixteen states and be trained in one tradition so that if they ever needed to protect this nation, they could protect it as one. This worked for about thirty years. But during the early 1830s, when Southern states became increasingly concerned about the antislavery movement, they met to discuss whether they might need to independently protect themselves against slave uprisings.

In 1778, the Virginia General Assembly had passed an act to create arsenals to store Virginia militia arms from the Revolutionary War and build a military academy to train officers. After the War of 1812, the Virginia militia had even more arms to store. The arsenal in Lexington was finally constructed in 1818, but a military academy for the state did not materialize.

Following the War of 1812, Congress debated the future of state militias and the regular army. On the one hand, Congress emphasized the poor performance of the state militias in the War of 1812 and the need for a regular professional force. On the other hand, some in Congress expressed fears that a strong US Army might carry out a coup d'état, overthrowing the newly formed national government, and argued that it might be better to have strengthened state militias that could be called upon.[26]

While historians are not sure how much these debates figured in the formation of VMI, it is apparent that the state of Virginia wanted to have its own citizen-soldiers and officers for the Virginia militia. A new military training institute could fulfill that desire. Graduating cadets would not be obliged to serve in the Virginia militia, but they could be called up when needed. Considering that this college-level training was the only military training of the day, graduates no doubt took their Virginia militia commissions seriously.

The Virginia militia still exists, and all VMI cadets are members. All VMI professors are given rank and wear the Virginia militia uniform on post, a US Army uniform with a gold pin that reads VA.

SLAVE REBELLIONS

VMI was formed in a time of fear in the South of slave rebellions. Just following the US independence from Great Britain, a successful slave rebellion took place in Haiti between 1791 and 1804. Slaves drove out the French plantation owners and sent shock waves through the slaveholding Southern United States.[27] Some plantation owners in the South were terrified that a similar rebellion might be organized against them. The economy of Virginia was based on tobacco farming, and the workforce was almost entirely slaves. Quakers, Methodists, and some Baptist congregations in the North and South were calling for the end of slavery, and antislavery movements in these churches were reaching preachers and congregations in African American churches north and south. Was a well-organized Virginia militia needed to put down a future possible slave rebellion?

Further stirring the pot over slavery were two presidents, George Washington and Thomas Jefferson, who were looking for a way to end slavery nationwide and freed some of their own slaves in their wills. George Washington (1732-99), having held slaves for fifty-six years, struggled with the morality of owning slaves and wrote of his desire to end the practice. In his 1799 will, he made the decision to free all his 123 enslaved people upon his death. Washington's wife, Martha Custis Washington, signed a deed of manumission for her husband's enslaved people in 1800 and released them on January 1, 1801. (The Custis estate owned an additional 153 people who could not be freed by George or Martha. Upon Martha's death in 1802, those people were divided among the Custis grandchildren.)[28]

Thomas Jefferson (1743-1826), who owned over 600 people over the course of his life, bought only twenty. The rest were inherited from his father and father-in-law or born on his estate. While Jefferson called slavery "a moral depravity" and a "hideous blot,"[29] he actively participated in slavery by buying and selling human beings, as the profits of his tobacco farming depended on this free labor. He publicly opposed slavery his entire life, saying it was the greatest threat to the survival of the new American nation. He said slavery was contrary to the laws of nature, and everyone had a right to personal liberty. His views were considered radical at the time. In

1778, Jefferson drafted a Virginia law that prohibited the importation of slaves by sea or land. (This law was passed by Congress in 1807 and went into effect January 1, 1808). In 1784, he proposed an ordinance to ban slavery in the Northwest territories. While Jefferson advocated for abolition through numerous proposals, the number of enslaved persons in Virginia skyrocketed from nearly 300,000 enslaved persons in 1790 to 470,000 in 1830. Slave labor was used primarily to cultivate tobacco. As soil depleted, the slaves became Virginia's most valuable commodity and important export. Jefferson warned that if slavery were not abolished, it could result in a civil war. During his lifetime, Jefferson freed five people, and another five were freed in his will. A remaining approximate 200 enslaved people were sold upon his death to pay debts.[30]

While Native Americans and the French had threatened the success of the new republic, the next very real threat was a slave uprising inspired by Haiti's Revolution. Gabriel Prosser, a slave on a plantation near Richmond, Virginia, plotted in 1800, with several other slaves, to seize parts of Richmond, burn houses, and kidnap Governor James Monroe. The plot was foiled when two coconspirators reported the plot. Twenty-six men, plus Gabriel Prosser, were arrested, convicted, and hanged.[31]

A second notable foiled uprising took place in Charleston, South Carolina, in 1822, led by a former slave, Denmark Vesey, whose statue now graces Hampton Park in Charleston. Vesey, a skilled carpenter, had won a lottery of $1,500 in 1799 and used the winnings to buy his freedom and set up his own successful business. A member of the American Methodist Episcopal Church, an African American church, he often used Biblical references to argue against slavery. Inspired by the Haitian Revolution, he planned, with numerous slaves, to escape, execute White enslavers, and then sail to Haiti. His elaborate plans were betrayed by two slaves who knew the plot.

Thirty-five men were hanged, including Vesey. The remarkable part of this story is what happened next. Fearful of more slave uprisings, ". . . white Charlestonians tore down the church and . . . Funds were appropriated to support a Municipal Guard of 150 men and the construction of 'a Citadel' to house them and weapons. In 1843, The Citadel structure became home to the cadets of the South Carolina Military Academy."[32] Today, it is known as The Citadel—The Military College of South Carolina, the military college most like VMI.

The third most frightening slave rebellion in the region was the one led by Nat Turner. Born in 1800 in Southampton County, Virginia, Nat was the child of a small plantation owner and a native African mother. In August 1831, Nat led the only effective, sustained slave rebellion in US history. His actions spread terror throughout the White South and set off a new wave of oppressive legislation prohibiting the education, movement, and assembly of slaves. It stiffened pro-slavery, anti-abolitionist convictions.

Nat had learned to read and write. Through time, he became increasingly religious, believing that God had appointed him, like Moses, to lead his people out of slavery. Slaves in nearby plantations began to call him "prophet." His plan was to seize arms from the county seat, aptly named Jerusalem, to kill White enslavers and move on to the Dismal Swamp, where capture would be difficult. He and seventy-five men killed about sixty Whites before the rebellion was put down by 3,000 Virginia militia soldiers. [33]

Thus, these three revolts of 1800, 1822, and 1831—plus calls for the abolition of slavery and the actions of Washington and Jefferson—no doubt were widely discussed and raised fears of a Haiti-like countrywide rebellion in the near future. It was in that Southern tension over slavery that VMI was formed. The proposal for the military school came about less than five years after Nat Turner's slave rebellion. The Virginia legislature was so shaken by this event that it considered gradually emancipating slaves in the state and removing them from Virginia to perhaps somewhere in Africa. Although we have no record of any local advocate of the school ever justifying the creation of VMI in the context of putting down a slave rebellion, Alden Partridge (1785-1854), an early superintendent of the West Point Military Academy, "advocated the development of state military schools in the South to prepare specifically for slave revolts."[34]

EQUAL SUFFRAGE FOR WHITE MEN

An important factor in the formation of VMI was western Virginia's quest for political influence through acquiring the right to vote for all White men. Why create another college for men when there were already other colleges for men in Virginia? There was The College of William and Mary in Williamsburg (1693), Hampton-Sydney College just outside of Farmville (1775), the University of Virginia in Charlottesville (1819), and Washington College (now Washington & Lee University, 1749 and 1813) located right beside the Lexington arsenal. None of these colleges, however, trained men to be military leaders.

Historian Jonson Miller investigated this question and concluded that the Scots-Irish and Germans of western Virginia, who were pushing for the formation of VMI, wanted to produce men who would be given respect for "self-mastery, morality, industriousness, and submission to lawful authority" that would prove their "equality or even moral superiority . . . over the sons of planters who attended Virginia's colleges." This would, in turn, result in achieving the right of these western men to vote and hold office, from which they were currently excluded.[35] Citizens of the Shenandoah Valley had no traditions of slaveholding and little political power because they lacked landownership.

Discussions around converting the arsenal into a college were taking place right after a Virginia Constitutional Convention in 1830 had failed to give voting rights to all White men in the state, something the disenfranchised had been pushing for. The right to vote was reserved for White male landowners or White men who rented substantially large farms. Landowners had argued that only they were men of virtue and had the education to vote wisely. Other White men, they argued, poorer men without land, would seek to vote in ways that would only serve their narrow self-interests. Thus, wealthy planters dominated political power. Western Virginians reasoned that non-landholding White men would gain more political power through professional training, especially in engineering.[36] Essentially, the military school proposal won out because of great dissatisfaction over limitations on who could vote in the state of Virginia.

By 1836, the Franklin Society argued that the new military school in Lexington would admit young men from poorer sections of society who would go through a disciplined and moral education that would make them fit for suffrage. Historian Jonson Miller concluded, "Expanded education would provide the means of achieving White manhood suffrage, shift political power westward, and secure internal improvements for western Virginia."[37] The requirement for men to own at least twenty-five dollars' worth of property to vote was dropped from the Virginia state constitution in 1850.

A NEED FOR ENGINEERS TO DEVELOP VIRGINIA

Another important motivation in the formation of VMI was the need for engineers to develop Virginia by creating a modern transportation system of railways and canals.

Claudius Crozet, a French engineer working for the state of Virginia in the 1820s and '30s, had noted repeatedly that Virginia lacked engineers to develop transportation necessary for economic development in the western part of the state. Crozet was well known for his surveys and attempts to get the legislature to fund transportation infrastructure that would expand the market economy of relatively isolated western Virginia. The new school would create engineers and teachers for the state.

FOUNDERS

★ ★ ★

"An investment in knowledge pays the best interest."
—Benjamin Franklin

"The philosophy of the school room in one generation will be the philosophy of government in the next."
—Abraham Lincoln

The state of Virginia had built the Lexington Arsenal in 1818 to store surplus munitions from the Revolutionary War and the War of 1812. It was manned by a captain, one or two corporals, and ten to thirteen privates.[38] It was one of three arsenals funded by the Virginia legislature in 1816.

Talk of converting the arsenal to a college or military school began with the Franklin Society, an intellectual discussion group in the town of Lexington, posing the question in their December 1834 meeting: "Would it be politic for the State to establish a military school, at the Arsenal, near Lexington, in connection with Washington College, on the plan of the West Point Academy?" After two discussion meetings, the society decided that the answer was "yes" and that they would "give the matter a practical shape." The arsenal was only sixteen years old, but the townspeople were not enamored with the young soldiers who guarded it. Altercations between the soldiers, who were not from the area, and town residents occurred often enough to engender complaints about the existence of the arsenal and soldiers. In May

1826, a fight between two soldiers resulted in a death. Although discipline at the arsenal was strict, how they made use of their leisure time was objectionable to the town's population.

PRESTON

When the Franklin Society decided in favor of converting the arsenal to a military college and replacing soldiers with students, one of its members, John Thomas Lewis Preston, wrote three articles in the *Lexington Gazette* to promote the idea to the public. He, and perhaps others, envisaged a four-year college where military life would dominate. Students would guard the arsenal and its store of weapons, but they would receive a liberal education in lieu of receiving any pay. The courses would include the "higher branches of an English education," sciences, and military art. The higher branches of an English education would include Latin, modern languages, and mathematics. Science would include natural philosophy and chemistry. One young man should be appointed to attend VMI from each senatorial district across the state. Preston presented this alternative vision to the townspeople:

> Who would not wish to see those really handsome buildings which, upon their commanding site, adorn the approach to our village, no longer the receptacle of drone, obliged to be restrained by coercion of military rule, a discordant element in our social system? But,
>
> The healthful and pleasant abode of a crowd of honorable youths pressing up the hill of science, with noble emulation, a gratifying spectacle, an honor to our country and our state, objects of honest pride to their instructors, and fare specimens of citizen-soldiers, attached to their native state, proud of her fame, and ready in every time of deepest peril to vindicate her honor or defend her rights.

But Preston's proposal was not the only proposal for converting the arsenal into some other kind of school to benefit society. Others in the town argued that funds should be diverted to establish a primary school, especially for children from poorer families. Another suggestion was to establish a school for the deaf so they could become productive members of society. More letters appeared in the local newspaper arguing the merits and flaws of each proposal. In the end, however, the proposal for a military school won out.

BARCLAY

From the beginning, Preston and others saw the US Military Academy at West Point as their model. This was perhaps brought about, in part, by a Lexington merchant, Mr. Hugh Barclay, who had visited West Point sometime in the early 1830s and was enormously impressed. A local widow asked Mr. Barclay if he could accompany her son to West Point, where he had been appointed as a cadet, and admit him, as Mr. Barclay was going North to buy goods for his store. His store was, in a sense, a clubhouse, and citizens of Lexington would come by in the evenings to swap news and discuss public affairs. Mr. Barclay acceded to the request. When he returned to Lexington, Barclay told the citizens of Lexington, with enthusiasm, what he had seen at West Point and that he favored converting the arsenal into a military school. In 1839, the governor appointed Mr. Barclay to the first VMI Board of Visitors (BOV), VMI's governing board.

CROZET

French engineer Claudius Crozet was VMI's first BOV president, and no doubt had an outsized influence on the formation of the Institute. As Virginia's principal engineer, he developed the engineering curriculum for the Institute. VMI remembers him today through the mess hall named Crozet Hall, built in 1935, and a landscaped monument completed in 2011, containing his burial site and headstone, with a bronze relief of Crozet. (Formerly, Crozet had been buried in front of the Preston Library from 1942 to 2007, with only a headstone.)

Crozet had studied engineering at the premier engineering school in Europe, if not the whole world—the École Polytechnique in Paris. It was a military-style school with strong discipline. After two years there, between the ages of fifteen and seventeen, Crozet went to officers' school and subsequently became a road and bridge engineer in Napoleon's army. Russia imprisoned him for two years. Upon his release from prison, he returned to Paris, where he asked for release from the French army. The army freed him from military service for a short time, and then Napoleon regained power, and Crozet was once again on active duty. He supported Napoleon as a new liberal leader, but after Napoleon's second abdication and the second restitution of the monarchy in France in 1815, Crozet had had enough of war and monarchs. He decided to emigrate to the new country—the United States of America. Crozet already had relatives in Louisiana, which may have influenced his decision.

On the ship to America with his new bride, Crozet met another French engineer on his way to work for the US Army and appointed to the BOV at West Point. It is probable that, through his influence, Crozet received an appointment in September 1816 to the engineering faculty at West Point to teach cadets destined for the US Army Corps of Engineers.

After seven years at West Point, frustrated with the administration, Crozet heard about a job opening in Virginia and applied to become Virginia's principal engineer. He served in this position from 1823-31, when he resigned to take a similar position in Louisiana. His time in Virginia had been frustrating. The legislature commissioned him to do a multitude of studies to improve transportation within the state, but most of the projects were never funded or underfunded. Engineers like to get things done, and Crozet felt the Virginia legislature would never fund the projects he designed.

In Louisiana, he met the same obstacles and had the same frustrations. The Louisiana legislature ordered detailed engineering studies for improving transportation and then would not fund them.

These legislators, who knew nothing of engineering or transportation, would offer him budgets at half the real cost, setting up projects for failure. Despite his earlier experience in Virginia, the governor of Virginia persuaded him to return in 1837 to take the position of principal engineer once again.[39] It was about this time that the new college of VMI was being envisioned, and Crozet became involved. His French military school training influenced how the military arts were to be taught, including even the design of cadet uniforms.

SMITH

With this vision, Preston recruited Francis H. Smith (1812–1890), a graduate of the US Military Academy at West Point, to be VMI's first superintendent. Smith was already living in Virginia, teaching at Hampton-Sydney College. Smith had served as a second lieutenant in the US Army from 1833 to 1836 and taught mathematics at West Point. He had resigned his commission to take a teaching position at Hampton-Sydney. A Virginian by birth, Smith gave his first loyalty to the state of Virginia. Sometime before the Civil War, he was sworn in as a colonel in the Virginia militia.

Smith served fifty years at VMI, from its opening in 1839 to 1889, guiding the dream of VMI becoming a Virginia military college. He brought to VMI his West Point training. Preston had envisaged a college to prepare citizen-soldiers with scientific training. Smith wanted to expand this to include agriculture, engineering, and fine arts. While Preston was concerned about the need for Virginia to have a military academy to train citizen-soldiers to "defend her rights," Smith felt that VMI should expand into a college of arts and sciences useful to the modernization of the state of Virginia.

In the fall of 1839, the new college of VMI enrolled twenty-three students in a three-year course and added six more students in January 1840. Classes began November 11, 1839, in outmoded arsenal quarters. In 1840, VMI added three new buildings to the post.

DAVIS—THE ARCHITECT
* ★ *

"America's greatest architect of the mid-nineteenth century, a designer of picturesque buildings in myriad styles . . ."
—Amelia Peck, The Metropolitan Museum of Art

The Lexington Arsenal was a small building, not suitable for more than a few cadets, and it lacked classrooms. To grow, VMI would need to be built like a college.

In the late 1840s, VMI contracted Alexander Jackson Davis (1803–1892) to draw up comprehensive architectural plans for the college, plans that would unfold for decades into the future. Indeed, VMI today still refers to those plans as it adds new buildings. His beautifully drawn and colorful plans reside in the VMI Archives and are available for viewing. I was awestruck the first time I saw them.

Davis was born in New York City. Having studied at the American Academy of Fine Arts and the National Academy of Design, he became one of the most successful and influential architects of his generation. He specialized in Greek Revival, Gothic Revival, and Italianate styles. VMI was the first American college planned entirely in Gothic Revival, a style that uses richly paned windows, towers, turrets, and other design elements found in medieval castles and cathedrals.

Davis became known to VMI through Philip St. George Cocke (1809–1861), a wealthy Virginia planter, slave owner, and member of the VMI BOV. At thirty-one, having inherited great wealth, Cocke employed Davis to design his residence, Belmead, in Powhatan

County, in the Gothic Revival style. The mansion is still standing. In the late 1840s, Philip St. George Cocke urged VMI to contract Davis to design the new campus.

Because the Cocke family exerted considerable influence on VMI from the 1840s through the 1930s, it seems worthwhile to digress to explore their history.

THE COCKE FAMILY

Like other wealthy Tidewater plantation owners, Philip Cocke was a descendant of a line of early English and Scottish immigrants to Virginia who were given land grants by the English Crown in return for helping to settle the land. In the early 1600s, the Virginia Company and King Charles I (owner of the Virginia colony) granted land or gave a "land patent" to anyone who wanted to start a plantation, awarding fifty acres of land "per head" who would work the land. The owner of the new plantation could acquire "headrights" by bringing over indentured workers from England, whose indentures usually lasted seven years, or by buying African slaves to work the land. The idea was to help empty out the poor and unemployed from an overcrowded London and create farms that would produce mostly tobacco for shipping back to England. It seemed like a win-win for the Virginia Company and the Crown because no gold or other minerals were found in Virginia, as had been hoped, but tobacco brought a good profit in England. The land was "free" because the company claimed that they had either discovered it or developed it, and therefore, it was their right to give away or sell it. Native Americans were consistently pushed off the land as the farms and plantations expanded. Over time, the system evolved into both giving away headrights and selling land. Wealthy Royalist supporters of Charles I brought enough wealth to Virginia to buy land from the Virginia Company as speculators and later sold it at a profit.

Philip St. George Cocke's ancestor, Richard Cocke, was one immigrant who took advantage of this new deal. He arrived in Virginia in 1627, and on March 6, 1636, the Virginia Company granted him 3,000 acres in Henrico County along the James River for transporting sixty immigrants, presumably indentured workers from England. In 1639, he acquired an additional 2,000 acres in Henrico County for transporting an additional forty persons. In 1652, he acquired another patent of 2,482 acres. Of these 7,482 acres from three patents, 622 acres were in an area that Cocke called "Bremo," where he had settled even before the first patent.*** It appears likely that Richard Cocke hailed from Shropshire, England, on the border with Wales.[40] Over time, the Cocke family grew and added plantations in Virginia and Mississippi by bringing over more indentured servants and supplementing their labor force with African slaves.

Richard Cocke's descendant, Philip St. George Cocke, who introduced VMI to the architect Davis, was born several generations later, in 1810, on the same Bremo Bluff plantation, in an early home on the site. After well over a century of cultivating their vast plantations, the Cocke family had fabulous wealth. Philip's father, John Hartwell Cocke (1780–1866), went on to build two more houses on the plantation, a Jacobean-style home at Bremo Recess around 1812 and a second plantation mansion in Palladian-style between 1812

***   Today, Bremo is in Fluvanna County, which was formed out of Henrico County in 1777. The origin of the name Bremo is not known, but the estate sits near a land patent owned by a Thomas Bremor, variously spelled Bremo, Bremoe, and other spellings. The land was known as the "Bremo dividend," an obsolete word meaning "share."

and 1819.††† Philip's father was a close friend of Thomas Jefferson, and the mansion was inspired by Jefferson's home. John H. Cocke and Jefferson experimented with better agricultural techniques and fretted together over how best to end slavery.

With his vast wealth, young Philip went on to acquire several more properties in Virginia and Mississippi. By 1860, at forty, he owned 27,000 acres in plantations and 610 slaves, and he estimated his net worth at 1 million dollars. (By comparison, George Washington, who is ranked 59 in the top 100 wealthiest Americans, owned a little over 7,000 acres in his farms associated with Mount Vernon and 123 slaves and had a net worth of $780,000 in 1799. But including land he bought for speculation, from New York to Virginia and west into Ohio and Kentucky, he owned a total of 52,000 undeveloped acres. Because of his land holdings, Washington is included in the 100 wealthiest Americans, whereas Philip St. George Cocke is not.)[41]

Importantly for the development of VMI, Philip Cocke had studied at the University of Virginia and graduated from the United States Military Academy at West Point in 1832. By 1840, he owned the family's plantation in Powhatan County, where he employed Davis to design his mansion. The governor appointed Philip to the VMI BOV in 1846, and he served in this capacity until 1852 and again from 1858 to 1861.

However, before his second term on the BOV was over, in 1861,

---

††† I tried to visit the historic Cocke homes of Bremo and Belmead, but neither is open to the public, and so I had limited success. The town of Bremo in Fluvanna County still exists, as does the Jacobean Cocke home built in 1812 on the plantation. The home and outbuildings can be viewed from a distance, but visitors are asked to leave. The Palladian mansion completed in 1819 still exists, but public access is not permitted, and I could not view it. In Powhatan County, the lengthy paved driveway to the Belmead mansion is also marked "private," but I was able to see the mansion briefly before being told that it had recently sold, and visitors were not welcome. This Gothic Revival home was in a poor state of repair and will likely be restored by the new owner.

his life ended in tragedy. In 1859, following John Brown's raid on Harper's Ferry—a raid that was intended to arm slaves in Virginia and incite a large slave revolt—Philip St. George Cocke had organized a local infantry group under the Virginia militia, called the Powhatan Troop, to defend against a potential slave uprising in Powhatan County. That troop, with Cocke as its head, joined the Confederate Army under General Robert E. Lee in April 1861. Having been a brigadier general in the Virginia militia, Cocke was highly insulted when Lee reduced his rank to colonel. After a period of protracted protest by Cocke, in October 1861, Lee agreed to raise Cocke's rank again to brigadier general. Following eight months of service during the first year of the Civil War that involved many harrowing battles, Cocke returned to Belmead, exhausted and still offended, to spend Christmas with his family. On December 26, 1861, at fifty-two, he committed suicide with his own pistol, leaving behind a wife and eleven children. Historians say that Cocke could not let go of his disdain for General Lee and the insult.[42]

Philip Cocke's suicide did not end the close relationship between VMI and the Cocke family. From 1856 to 1945, sixteen VMI graduates had the surname Cocke, and two more graduates had the middle name Cocke. Philip's son, also named Philip St. George Cocke, graduated from VMI in 1866.[43] William H. Cocke (1874–1938), an 1894 graduate of VMI, served as superintendent of the Institute from 1924 to 1929.[44] However, based on genealogical research by the family, William Cocke is not directly related to Philip St. George Cocke.[45] In 1926, a new building containing a gymnasium was dedicated as Cocke Hall in recognition of a generous personal gift from Cocke for the construction of the building.[46]

As this long and winding story shows, this aura of honor at VMI prior to the Civil War was tied to the Gothic architecture of the Institute buildings, and that architecture was inspired and executed by one of Virginia's oldest plantation families, the Cockes, a family that had much to lose should the old system of slavery fall.

THE WASHINGTON STATUE

After construction of the first phase of the architectural plan was built, the state of Virginia, in 1856, purchased and gifted to VMI a bronze replica of the famous marble statue of George Washington by Jean-Antoine Houdon, the original of which stands in the rotunda of the Virginia State Capitol in Richmond.[47] (The sculptor, William Hubard, envisioned selling copies of the statue to each of the original thirteen colonies.) Superintendent Smith was very pleased; he constantly looked for ways to keep George Washington in front of cadets. Washington's likeness is also on the VMI diploma and the corps flag.[48] Superintendent Smith was an admirer of George Washington. He even lobbied to have VMI moved to Mt. Vernon, the former home of George Washington in Northern Virginia.[49] The statue currently stands on the parapet facing the south side of the barracks. The span of barracks opposite this statue is entered through the Washington Arch.

Like other artists whose works grace VMI, William James Hubard (1807–1862) was internationally known and connected to Tidewater planters. Born in England, Hubard was a magnificent painter who lived and painted in Europe and the eastern states of the US. As a boy, he had traveled around England with a performing troop, cutting and selling silhouettes. In 1824, the manager of the performing troop brought him to New York, where he took up portrait painting. In the 1830s, he moved to Virginia and, in 1837, married the daughter of a wealthy Tidewater family. The couple went to Europe for two years for William to study painting and returned by 1839. Around 1850, he moved his family permanently to Richmond, Virginia, and became interested in sculpture. He owned nine slaves. He built a studio and foundry outside of Richmond, where he made six copies of the Houdon statue of Washington. He sold only one copy, presumably the VMI statue, coming near to financial ruin. So, with the approach of the Civil War, he refitted his factory to make Brooke rifles for the

Confederacy. (The other five statues each now sit in a new location: the Smithsonian, the US Capitol, the North Carolina State Capitol, Miami University, and the city of St. Louis.)[50]

Nearly twenty years after VMI was established, there was still ongoing discussion about what the Institute should be or become. In 1858, Frances Smith took a trip to Europe to look at institutions with a scientific and military character. He was impressed with the École Polytechnique in France, the greatest military technical school, the school that Claudius Crozet had attended. In 1859, he sent a report to the General Assembly of Virginia "recommending that VMI be organized as a general scientific school, with three special schools of application: one, agriculture; two, engineering; and three, fine arts."[51] This was two years before the states that would become the Confederacy seceded from the Union, and Lincoln was elected president of the United States, the event that set off the formation of the Confederacy. Smith was focused on academic excellence and probably could not imagine the Union breaking apart or his cadets going to war.

THE CIVIL WAR PERIOD
★ ★ ★

"The Institute will be heard from today."
—General Thomas "Stonewall" Jackson at the Battle of Chancellorsville, 1863

THE STORM BREWS

From 1839 to 1859, VMI trained hundreds of cadets, and all alumni were Virginians. At that time, all allegiance was first to one's state. This explains why, in 1861, after Virginia secedes from the Union and joins the Confederacy, VMI faculty and cadets began joining the Army of Northern Virginia.

Many of the earliest graduates served as officers in the Mexican–American War, 1846-48, and others had served as militia inspectors.[52] Training at VMI was broader and more academic than at West Point and aimed not to just produce military officers but professional men who could also serve as officers in times of need. As the state of Virginia provided most of the funds and scholarships for the Institute, students from outside Virginia were not admitted until 1858.

The storm over slavery continued to brew. The freed slave Frederick Douglass, along with several antislavery groups in the North, pressed for the abolition of slavery. Abolitionist literature circulated in the North and South. The Underground Railroad was ferrying escaped slaves from the South to the North. In 1854, with the passing of the Kansas-Nebraska Act, conflict arose over whether the territory would become slaveholding or not. In fact, the dispute revolved around whether any new state could be a slaveholding state.

VMI AT JOHN BROWN'S HANGING

The militant abolitionist John Brown (1800–1859) was fanatical about advocating for the territory to be free of slavery.

For years, Brown had participated in the Underground Railroad, gave land to freed slaves, and established the League of Gileadites, which sought to protect escaped slaves from slave hunters. Battles ensued in the territory between hastily assembled pro-slavery and antislavery forces. John Brown and his sons entered the fighting, and in 1856, they killed five pro-slavery settlers. But Brown believed that the only way to free the slaves was to arm them for a major uprising in which they would fight for their freedom. In October 1859, Brown led a contingent of twenty-one men on a failed raid on Harper's Ferry Federal Armory in Virginia (now in West Virginia). He sought to steal weapons to arm slaves and set off a rebellion, but his sons were killed, and he was captured and sentenced to death in November. The raid on Harper's Ferry was a pivotal moment in American history, and historians credit this event as being a main trigger for the Civil War.[53]

Brown was to be hung in Charles Town. Henry Wise, the governor of Virginia, had the authority to commute Brown's sentence to life in prison, and many abolitionists begged for this. But Wise refused. Rumors started flying that hundreds of abolitionists were on their way to Charles Town to rescue Brown. Consequently, Wise asked VMI Superintendent Colonel Smith to bring a contingent of VMI cadets to the hanging to ensure there were no riots or attempts to rescue the prisoner. Twelve faculty and staff, including the young Professor Thomas Jonathan Jackson and Professor John Preston, led eighty-three VMI cadets to Charles Town to provide security around the execution on December 2, 1859.[54] Governor Wise also appointed Colonel Smith "superintendent" of the execution—and to give the execution order. (John Wilkes Booth, Lincoln's assassin, also attended the execution.) The prominent and fiery Southern nationalist Edmund Ruffin, who had spent his life defending slavery, joined the VMI group.[55] Witnessing this execution with Superintendent Smith, Professor Jackson, Professor Preston, and this firebrand Virginia planter must have been a life-altering event for the young cadets. The message was clear: insurrection against slavery was treason.

VMI AND EDMUND RUFFIN

The wealthy Virginia plantation owner Edmund Ruffin had close ties with the Institute. Planters in the South considered him to be the father of soil science, as he wrote extensively on agriculture. Tobacco depleted the soil of nutrients; his writing focused on techniques to help recover soil health. In the late 1850s, Superintendent Smith wanted to establish a school of agriculture at VMI and asked Ruffin to head the new school.[56] However, this did not happen because Ruffin had his own higher cause to focus on. Like most prominent Virginia men, Ruffin had served in the Virginia militia. His family owned 200 slaves, and Ruffin was convinced that the South would have to secede from the Union to maintain the chattel slavery system. He lobbied officials and produced publications advocating Southern nationhood. After the hanging of John Brown, Ruffin ceded his land to his children and devoted himself full-time to traveling the South to promote secession.[57]

Ruffin's ancestry, like that of Philip St. George Cocke, goes back to the year 1635 when William Ruffin migrated to Virginia and settled in Isle of Wight County. Over time, he and his descendants expanded their land holdings to become one of the wealthier families in Virginia.[58] Genealogies show that the Ruffins intermarried with members of a Cocke family. Between 1852 and 1943, fourteen cadets with the surname Ruffin attended VMI, including Edmund Ruffin's son, Charles, who graduated in 1852.[59]

SOUTHERN STATES SECEDE

Following the election and inauguration of Abraham Lincoln, from December 20, 1860, through June 1861, Virginia and ten other slaveholding Southern states had followed Ruffin's exhortations and seceded from the Union of the United States of America. Although Lincoln detested slavery, during his election period, he had vowed not to oppose it if elected president. On the other hand, he did vow not to allow future states that entered the Union to be slaveholding. This presidential promise was crucial to the Southern states' decision to withdraw from the Union; they saw it as a threat to their future and decided it was better to form a loose Confederation of States that would no longer be ruled by a strong central government.

The leaders of many slaveholding states dreamed of expanding their investments in plantations westward into Kansas, Nebraska, and farther and southward into Mexico, Central America, and Brazil, which would all be slaveholding states with large plantations. They would make their own laws, state by state, to suit their individual circumstances. Some, such as South Carolina and Georgia, envisaged becoming independent countries comprising large plantations.

Among those advocating for the expansion of slavery into a new slave state of Brazil was a certain Matthew Fontaine Maury (1806–1873), founder of the US Naval Observatory and modern oceanography and, later, professor at VMI from 1868 until his death five years later. The Maury-Brooke Hall at VMI is named after him; his birthday used to be a Virginia school holiday. And the Maury River flows through Lexington. Maury is another VMI connection to the Confederacy, and his way of thinking reveals what tangles of logic ensnared people attempting to save the Southern slave system. As Charles C. Mann explains in his book, *1493*,

> An ardent advocate of slavery, Maury became possessed in the 1850s by the fear that the South would lose its political clout because it was not big enough to withstand the North.

In a widely circulated pamphlet, he proposed a solution: The United States should annex the Amazon basin. Ocean currents push the river's outflow into the Caribbean, where it meets the outflow from the Mississippi—proof, to Maury's mind, that the Amazon was, oceanographically speaking, part of North America, not South America. For this reason, he argued, the Amazon valley was a natural "safety valve for our Southern States." He set two cartographers to map Amazonia for the future day when US slaveholders would go "with their goods and chattels to settle and to revolutionize and to republicanize and Anglo Saxonize that valley." Southern plantation owners should resettle there, Maury argued, converting the river basin into the biggest US slave State. Few planters paid attention until the South lost the Civil War. Hoping to re-create slave society in the forest, ten thousand Confederates fled to the Amazon. All but a few hundred quickly fled back. The remaining die-hards formed a sort of micro-satellite of the Confederacy in the town of Santarem, in the lower Amazon.[60]

The Confederate States of America formed a government and drew up a constitution that read almost exactly the same as the US Constitution except that member states were forbidden to pass legislation prohibiting slavery, and all future territories or states that joined the Confederacy would have the right to institute and maintain slavery: *"In all such territory, the institution of negro slavery as it now exists in the Confederate States, shall be recognized and protected by Congress, and by the territorial government."*

Lincoln wanted to save the Union, and to do so, he was willing to ignore the question of slavery, although he personally opposed it. When it became evident that the Confederacy was willing to fight a war for their independence, Frederick Douglass and many others pressed for Lincoln to free the slaves so they could join the Northern army and help win a war against the South. Lincoln refused until 1863. The president repeatedly said that this was not a war over slavery but a war to hold the United States of America together. But most people knew that the underbelly of the war was the question of slavery.

CADETS AND FACULTY LEAVE TO FIGHT

VMI became increasingly caught up in this strife. Virginia was the largest slaveholding state in the South. People in Virginia thought of Virginia as their "country" and placed their loyalty to the state above their loyalty to the United States. Even though Virginia had produced seven US presidents who served between 1789 and 1849 (Washington, Jefferson, Madison, Monroe, Harrison, Tyler, and Taylor), their first loyalty was to Virginia.

By the time the Civil War started, VMI had grown to over 250 student cadets, ages fifteen to twenty-five. By 1860, VMI had graduated 2,000 cadets. By 1861, faculty, graduates, and students began joining the Confederate Army, mostly out of loyalty to their state. This level of loyalty was seen also in Robert E. Lee, a graduate of the United States Military Academy at West Point, New York. He turned down Lincoln's offer to lead the Union Army and accepted an offer from Confederate president Jefferson Davis to lead the Confederate Army while confessing that he did not believe in secession or slavery—he simply owed his loyalty to his "country" of Virginia. He could not fight against his home state. Other Virginians felt the same way, as did most of the cadets and faculty at VMI.

According to VMI Archives, "Of the 1,930 alumni who were living at the beginning of the Civil War, 1,827 (94.7%) served in the Southern and Northern armies. Of those, 240 died (two-thirds killed or mortally wounded and one-third from other causes). Approximately nineteen served in the Union Army."[61]

Natural philosophy‡‡‡ professor Thomas Jonathan Jackson left

---

‡‡‡ Natural philosophy was close to modern-day physics and optics.

the Institute in 1861 to join the Confederate Army and took with him all but forty-seven younger cadets, those left behind to guard the Institute. However, eight months later, most of these joined their fellow cadets at Camp Lee in Richmond. While students, cadets were exempt from conscription, yet most left VMI to join the Confederate States Army. These young cadets trained and drilled as many as 15,000 to 20,000 Confederate soldiers. VMI graduates took many of the commanding posts. During the Civil War, twenty-two men who had taught at or attended VMI achieved the rank of general in the Confederate Army, nearly 300 became field officers, and more than 500 acted as company-grade officers. "So many served under Jackson that just before his famous flank attack on the Union Army at Chancellorsville in 1863, the general said, 'the Institute will be heard from today.'"[62]

Students continued to enroll at VMI in 1861, 1862, and 1863, and during these years, they were called upon by the state of Virginia. Virginia Governor Pierpont asked General Smith to send VMI cadets to join Confederate forces in May 1862 in active duty but faced no fire. In May 1863, he summoned them to accompany Stonewall Jackson's body for burial in the Lexington cemetery. From August through December 1863, they were called up for active duty. To this point, no cadet had faced battle or died from service.

BATTLE OF NEW MARKET AND BURNING OF VMI

In mid-May 1864, Confederate Commanding Officer John C. Breckinridge called upon VMI's 257 cadets to join Confederate forces to defend against an advancing federal army under Union General Franz Sigel that was proceeding down the Shenandoah Valley. These young men marched for four days, some eighty-five miles, to New Market, Virginia, where, exhausted, they fought. Breckinridge had planned to keep the cadets as a reserve force because, it is said, he viewed them as children. Indeed, the youngest was fifteen. But these cadets made a valiant charge against Union forces. Ten lost their lives, and forty-five were wounded. Confederate forces won the battle, and leaders credited the cadets with helping to achieve this victory. A deeply muddy section of the battlefield came to be called the "Field of Lost Shoes" because so many cadets had lost their boots to the sticky muck. *Field of Lost Shoes* is also the title of a full-length motion picture and dramatization of this epic event, released in 2014. The Battle of New Market was the only time VMI cadets participated in a battle, yet much of VMI glory and lore centers around this battle.

A month later, on June 12, 1864, Union Major General David Hunter, West Point Class of 1822, burned the Institute, shelled Lexington, and ransacked Washington College. Just before the arrival of the Union Army, cadets had been evacuated toward Lynchburg. When the Union troops burned the barracks, they also took VMI's statue of George Washington, justifying the act by claiming that VMI had turned its back on the United States and did not deserve to own it. Union troops took the statue to the new state of West Virginia (formed in 1861), a Union state, to adorn its capitol in Charleston.

VMI REBUILDS

VMI reopened in October 1865, after the end of the Civil War, with Smith continuing as the superintendent. After much negotiation, Charleston returned the Washington statue, and VMI rededicated it in 1866.

VMI welcomed at least three prominent former Confederate officers to become faculty at VMI soon after the war ended. George Washington Custis Lee, West Point Class of 1854, son of Confederate General Robert E. Lee, joined in 1865 at about the same time his father accepted an appointment as President of Washington College. John Mercer Brooke, oceanographer and scientist, US Naval Academy Class of 1847, joined in 1865. As mentioned earlier, Matthew Fontaine Maury, astronomer, historian, oceanographer, meteorologist, cartographer, and geologist, joined in 1868.

No doubt, many large plantation owners, generals, and officers of the Confederate States Army were distraught at the victory of the Northern Army over its Southern counterpart. One of those was Edmund Ruffin. So deep was his ardor for a Confederacy of States independent of the Union and the continuation of slavery that, in 1865, when General Lee surrendered in Appomattox, Virginia, Ruffin committed suicide at seventy-one. Just before his death, he left the following note:

> And now with my latest writing and utterance, and with what will [be] near to my latest breath, I here repeat, & would willingly proclaim, my unmitigated hatred to Yankee rule—to all political, social and business connections with Yankees, & to the perfidious, malignant, & vile Yankee race.[63]

It is impressive that VMI was not defeated by the loss of the war and the destruction of many of the buildings. The Institute embarked on a period of rebuilding while honoring cadets who died at the Battle of New Market and fallen Professor General Jackson. Yet, with at least five of its faculty being former Confederate officers, the atmosphere at VMI must have been holding on to a lost cause.

POST-CIVIL WAR MEMORIALS

★ ★ ★

"The only way human beings can win a war is to prevent it."
—General George C. Marshall, Class of 1901

Having been partially burned down in 1864 by Union forces—and having lost ten cadets in the Battle of New Market—VMI turned its attention to rebuilding and rededicating itself to providing a military and liberal arts education. But the pain and the pride of VMI's role in the Civil War would not go away. For the next 100 years, VMI mirrored a larger Southern movement to keep the memory of the Confederacy alive. But these were not the only memorials that VMI built. VMI also honored alumni who died in foreign wars and famous alumni George C. Marshall and Jonathan Daniels.

Although Southerners began honoring the Confederacy by erecting statues and displaying other symbols right at the end of the Civil War, the dedication of large monuments and memorials rose significantly in two distinct periods across the South. The first was around 1900, the time when Southern states began enacting Jim Crow laws to disenfranchise African Americans and resegregate society, and it lasted into the late 1920s, a period of dramatic resurgence of the Ku Klux Klan nationwide. The second escalation occurred from the early 1950s through the 1960s as a backlash to the Civil Rights Movement.[64] Memorials at VMI followed roughly the same pattern.

There was a first peak of Confederate remembrance from the late 1880s to the 1920s and a second peak from the 1950s to the 1970s. In between these two periods, VMI constructed memorials to all its alumni, especially those who died in foreign wars—and especially to George C. Marshall.

FIRST PEAK OF CONFEDERATE REMEMBRANCE—1880S TO 1920S

Two years after the Battle of New Market, in 1866, VMI ceremoniously brought the remains of five fallen cadets to Lexington and, after religious services, placed them in a vault. Twelve years later, in 1878, VMI again ceremoniously interred them in a newly created Cadet Cemetery, which is now part of the parade ground. (The Cadet Cemetery no longer exists). That same year, VMI established a formal ceremony to be held annually every May 15, the day of the Battle of New Market, to honor these fallen cadets. This ceremony still takes place today to commemorate not only the cadets at the Battle of New Market but also all alumni who have served and died in time of war.[65]

Fifteen years later, from 1893 to 1896, the VMI BOV decided to build a memorial hall for their famous Confederate General, Thomas Jonathan "Stonewall" Jackson. A graduate of the United States Military Academy at West Point and one of the best-known Confederate generals (after Robert E. Lee), Jackson taught at VMI from 1851 until 1861, when he joined the Confederate Army. At VMI, Jackson was responsible for the Department of Natural and Experimental Philosophy (today, the Physics Department). According to historians, he was not a particularly popular professor. His fame derives from his prominent role in the Civil War.

The biggest spike in Confederate memorials nationwide came during the early 1900s. Largely spearheaded by the United Daughters of the Confederacy (UDC), more than 400 monuments were erected throughout the South to reshape Civil War history as a glorious lost cause.

And so, it happened at VMI as well.

Thirty years after the end of the Civil War, VMI began greater efforts to bring its Confederate heroes to the fore. As mentioned above, in 1896, VMI built a chapel adjacent to the cadet barracks and named it Jackson Memorial Hall. Virginia artist Benjamin West Clinedinst (1859–1931), a member of the Class of 1880, donated a painting of the Battle of New Market, designed for the chapel apse, showing VMI cadets making their charge against the Northern forces. The painting was installed and unveiled in 1914. Clinedinst studied in Baltimore and Paris and became well-known in the art world. VMI demolished Jackson Memorial Hall in 1915 because it conflicted with the original design for the expansion of the cadet barracks. They rebuilt it east of the barracks in 1916. The painting was reinstalled in the new chapel. The building continues to serve as the interdenominational chapel, with 1,150 seats. In 2020, the VMI BOV voted to remove Jackson's name from Memorial Hall and from the Jackson Arch as part of several Institute reforms.

Soon after the construction of the first Jackson Memorial Hall, in 1903, an 1866 graduate, Moses J. Ezekiel, who had fought in the Battle of New Market as a cadet, donated a remarkable monument in bronze called *Virginia Mourning Her Dead* to honor those cadets who died at New Market. It was erected in front of VMI barracks at the head of the parade ground, the most central and noticeable position on post. And then again, in 1912, the highest point in the erection of Confederate monuments throughout the United States, Ezekiel donated a second memorial, a bronze statue of Stonewall Jackson. *Virginia Mourning Her Dead* was moved to the east side of the parade ground to make room for the Jackson statue. The remains of the five fallen cadets were moved once again and buried beneath *Virginia Mourning Her Dead*, now called the New Market Memorial. (In 1960, the remains of a sixth fallen cadet were added). Symbolic headstones for the other four cadets sit behind the monument.

The statue of General Thomas Jonathan "Stonewall" Jackson now occupied the most important spot on post from 1912 to December 2020. The statue was flanked on either side by the four cannons of the 1848 Cadet Battery. The statue is a replica of the one that Moses Ezekiel made for the city of Charleston, West Virginia. Just behind Jackson's statue was the Jackson Arch, where a quotation that Jackson loved is carved into stone: "You may be whatever you resolve to be."

Moses Jacob Ezekiel (1844–1917) is no doubt one of VMI's most famous graduates. Born to a Jewish Spanish immigrant family from Richmond, Virginia, he was VMI's first Jewish cadet. His grandparents had emigrated from Holland, where his ancestors had arrived 400 years earlier to escape the Spanish Inquisition.

Ezekiel had attended school until age twelve and then began working in his step-grandfather's store as a bookkeeper. When he realized that he needed an education, he applied to VMI for a State Cadetship. He had been creating art from about the age of thirteen, and when he arrived at VMI, he began portraiture there. After the Civil War, General Robert E. Lee, who had become president of Washington and Lee College, recognized his talent and encouraged him to pursue a career in art. The VMI Archives has several drawings that Ezekiel made of his professors and three female slaves at his home in Richmond. He fought in the Battle of New Market, helped to identify and collect bodies after the battle, and nursed a cadet descendant of Thomas Jefferson in a New Market home for two days until Cadet Jefferson's death. He was also present at the funeral of Stonewall Jackson in 1863 as a casket guard, all these experiences moving him to compassion for those who had lost their lives in the Civil War.

After graduation, Ezekiel studied sculpture in Berlin and became a prolific sculptor. He spent the rest of his life in Rome, where he received numerous awards from royalty and art societies for his spectacular work. An ardent supporter of the Confederacy until his death in 1917, he accepted a commission by the UDC to create the Confederate Memorial for Arlington National Cemetery, unveiled in

1914. At his request, he is buried at the foot of this memorial. In 2022, it was slated by the Pentagon to be removed, an action supported by more than twenty of his descendants, as early as 2017, calling it "a relic of a racist past."[66] It was removed in December 2023.

In 1931, a statue of Major General Francis H. Smith was added on post. Because Smith had served as a major general in the Virginia militia and a colonel in the Confederate States Army, some consider his statue also to be a Confederate statue.[67] However, at VMI, most faculty and cadets assert that the Smith statue honors the man who served as VMI's superintendent for fifty years. The statue sits in front of Smith Hall, VMI's administration building, facing the parade ground and barracks, nearly opposite the Jackson statue before removal in December 2020. Smith is depicted in his VMI faculty uniform and has a diploma in one hand and a Bible in the other. Upon graduation, he handed every VMI cadet a Bible inscribed with a verse he thought appropriate to each cadet. And because he is wearing spectacles, he is affectionately called "Old Specs." The statue was created by Italian-born sculptor Ferrucio Legnaioli. He had emigrated from Florence, Italy, to New York City in 1902, and Italian friends in Richmond coaxed him to move to Richmond in 1907. Works of Legnaioli decorated the National Theater and many homes and buildings in Richmond.

While the memory of VMI's brief but spectacular role in the Civil War was being preserved and glorified during this first spike of Confederate memorials, there remained a focus at VMI and in the state legislature to produce outstanding citizen-soldiers—VMI's original reason for existence. In 1913, the 'Society of Cincinnatus' in Virginia created a fund for a Cincinnatus medal, an award given to the VMI graduating cadet who "has demonstrated to the greatest degree excellence of character and efficient of service."[68] The medal is named after Lucius Quinctius Cincinnatus (born 519 BCE), a Roman statesman who gained fame for his selfless devotion to the republic in times of crisis and for giving up the reins of power when the crisis was over. When George Washington gave up leadership of the Continental Army following the American Revolution, American leaders compared him to Cincinnatus. Continental Army soldiers formed The Cincinnatus Society, a fraternity of veterans, in 1783, and Washington was elected its first president. A Cincinnatus monument was added on post in 1983, listing the names of all awardees since 1913.

HONORING ALUMNI AND GEORGE C. MARSHALL

In April 1917, the United States entered World War I, and VMI graduates were among those who served. In 1928, to honor all those VMI graduates who had died in wars up to the end of WWI and to honor her husband, Anne Cocke, wife of former Superintendent William H. Cocke, donated funds to the Institute to build a Memorial Garden in front of the then new Cocke Hall, VMI's gymnasium.

Brigadier General William Horner Cocke (1874-1938) graduated from VMI in 1894. Cocke served as a US Army officer in both the Spanish-American War and World War I and as VMI's fourth superintendent from 1924 to 1929. The construction of Cocke Hall was made possible by Gen. Cocke's significant donation toward the cost of construction. Cocke Hall served until 2019 as the main athletic building.

On the walls of the stairway leading to the sunken Memorial Garden hang bronze tablets placed in memory of deceased cadets and alumni, as well as the famous quote by VMI founder Colonel J. T. L. Preston:

> THE HEALTHFUL AND PLEASANT ABODE OF A CROWD OF HONORABLE YOUTHS PRESSING UP THE HILL OF SCIENCE: WITH NOBLE EMULATION A GRATIFYING SPECTACLE: AN HONOR TO OUR COUNTRY AND OUR STATE: OBJECTS OF HONEST PRIDE TO THEIR INSTRUCTORS AND FAIR

SPECIMENS OF CITIZEN SOLDIERS: ATTACHED TO THEIR NATIVE STATE PROUD OF HER FAME AND READY IN EVERY TIME OF DEEPEST PERIL TO VINDICATE HER HONOR OR DEFEND HER RIGHTS.
COLONEL J.T.L. PRESTON

In 1939, Anne Cocke enhanced the Memorial Garden with a beautifully sculpted white marble statue of a nude young man, titled *Spirit of Youth*, by Tuscan-born sculptor Attilio Piccirilli (1866–1945). Like other artists whose works grace VMI, Piccirilli was a world-renowned artist. He studied sculpture at the Academia San Luca in Rome from 1881 to 1888 and then emigrated to New York City with his parents and five brothers in 1887. His father and brothers set up a studio in the Bronx in 1893, where they took commissioned work and produced sculptures for sale, working in white marble. Today, their works are in museums, such as the Metropolitan Museum of Art, and found throughout New York City and beyond.[69] Their best-known project is the 19-foot statue of Abraham Lincoln in the Lincoln Memorial in Washington, DC. Their workshop became one of the most famous sculpting studios in America at the time, and many famous sculptors and political figures, including Teddy Roosevelt and John D. Rockefeller, visited it. Piccirilli was a cofounder of the Leonardo da Vinci Art School, which offered art education to thousands of working-class New Yorkers from 1923 to 1940.

The *Spirit of Youth* statue has an interesting oral history that is difficult to verify. According to a VMI Museum leaflet, Italian dictator Benito Mussolini originally commissioned the statue. Piccirilli refused to ship the statue to Italy in protest of Mussolini's fascist policies and Hitler. When General and Mrs. Cocke visited Piccirilli's New York studio somewhere around 1937 or 1938, looking for an appropriate statue for the Memorial Garden, the sculptor offered to sell them the statue.[70]

The Memorial Garden was designed by nationally recognized landscape architect Ferruccio Vitale (1875–1933). Vitale was born and raised in Florence, Italy, and studied landscape architecture there and in Turin and Paris. He emigrated to the United States in 1902 and became an American citizen in 1921. Vitale designed other well-known gardens, such as the National Mall, the Washington Monument Gardens, the National Gallery of Art, and many others up and down the East Coast. It is likely that Anne Cocke met Vitale through the Garden Club of Virginia.[71] All cadets pass through this garden on the way to Cocke Hall and some of the athletic fields. VMI holds various cadet and alumni functions there, such as class reunions and memorial services for departed classmates.

From the early 1930s to the early 1960s, VMI constructed several additional buildings, including a New Barracks (1949), using the architect Davis's 1849 blueprints, but no additional statues or monuments of note. VMI honored its most famous graduate, General George C. Marshall, Class of 1901, by naming the arch into New Barracks the Marshall Arch (1951).

A five-star general during World War II, Marshall was the US Army Chief of Staff, US Secretary of State following the war, and architect of the reconstruction of Europe, better known as the Marshall Plan. In 1947, Marshall proposed that the United States provide economic assistance to restore the economic infrastructure of postwar Europe. On April 3, 1948, President Truman signed the Economic Recovery Act of 1948. Recognized around the world for its wisdom, Sweden awarded Marshall the Nobel Peace Prize in 1953. In 1964, The George C. Marshall Foundation built a memorial museum and library dedicated to Marshall. In 1978, VMI erected a bronze statue of Marshall in front of the Marshall Arch. The VMI Foundation raised funds for the statue, and a VMI graduate, Aldolfo Ponzanelli, Class of 1932, turned to his friend, Augusto Bozzano, a sculptor, to create the statue.[72]

In 2001, VMI created the George C. Marshall Citizen-Soldier

Award, given biannually to a 1st Class cadet or rising 1st Class cadet who best models the attributes displayed by George C. Marshall.[73]

This recognition of Marshall's historic role in and after World War II—and VMI alumni who died in WW II—diminished VMI's focus on its historical Civil War orientation. More cadets from outside Virginia began attending VMI. Historians Deetz et al. capture the essence of this shift: "After World War II, VMI turned to Marshall and other former cadets who served in the war, placed them at the center of a historical saga . . ." [74]

One final sculpture at VMI worthy of mention is tucked to one side of the entrance to the VMI Museum in the lower level of Jackson Memorial Hall. It is a beautifully crafted painted plaster interpretation of Saint Francis of Assisi by William Marks Simpson, VMI Class of 1924. Created in 1927, this sculpture won the famous Prix de Rome, a scholarship for art students, in 1930. Simpson taught sculpture at VMI in the 1950s.

SECOND PEAK OF CONFEDERATE REMEMBRANCE—1950S THROUGH 1970S

The second peak of remembrance of the Civil War at VMI began in the 1950s and ran through the 1970s. In 1957, the UDC created The Stonewall Jackson Memorial Award, presented annually to the first standing graduate in the physics curriculum. In 2022, the VMI BOV voted to end this award.

In 1971, VMI began holding a ceremony in New Market, Virginia, every September to honor the cadets who fought in the Battle of New Market, and where, beginning in 1996, rats took their "oath of cadetship." They listened to talks on overcoming unexpected and seemingly impossible challenges.[75] The event was attended by family and friends of rats, sometimes reaching 2,000 people. Every incoming class of rats rode a caravan of buses to New Market to attend the ceremony, where, as part of the ceremony, they reenacted the cadet charge against Federal troops. This tradition continued until 2020, when VMI decided to change it to a celebration of the sacrifice of all graduates who have died in all our nation's wars. They stopped reenacting the Battle of New Market, officially due to COVID-19, but no doubt also due to negative press in a national atmosphere of racial reckoning.[76]

In 1985, the Virginia Division of the UDC established the Commodore Matthew Fontaine Maury Award in memory of the famed oceanographer, meteorologist, supporter of the Confederacy, and former member of the VMI faculty from 1868 until 1872. The award is made annually to the first-ranking graduate in the mathematics curriculum.[77]

In 2009, the UDC was still working to keep alive the memories of what they consider to be Confederate heroes. That year, they created the Sir Moses Ezekiel Award to be given annually "to a cadet whose accomplishments in such areas of the humanities as visual arts, the theater arts, music, literature, history and museology have significantly enriched the cultural lives of his or her fellow cadets and enhanced the reputation of VMI." The award is not a VMI award, but VMI allows the UDC to give the award to a student selected by the dean of faculty. Like the Jackson award, in 2022, the VMI BOV voted to terminate the Sir Moses Ezekiel Award, but the award was reinstated in 2023.[78]

As late as 2013, VMI's Class of 1964 created the New Market Legacy Award. It is presented annually to a 1st Class cadet whose cadetship—in the opinion of his or her brother rats—is most reflective of the character, honor, and spirit of the 1864 New Market Corps of Cadets.[79]

These awards are not VMI's total focus when it comes to memorials. VMI also honors all alumni who ever served in a war. Their names are listed on plaques attached to barracks.

It is truly awesome to reflect upon the amazing works of art created by VMI graduates—Ezekiel (Class of 1866), Clinedinst (Class of 1880), Simpson (Class of 1924)—together with the creations of other internationally recognized artists, architects, and designers—

Davis, Legnaioli, Vitale, Piccirilli, and Hubard. Daily, cadets in the Class of '68 were surrounded by creations of some of the greatest nineteenth- and twentieth-century artists in America. In 1968, the Battle of New Market, *Virginia Mourning Her Dead*, the statues of Washington, Jackson, and Smith, and Memorial Garden, with its Spirit of Youth statue, dominated the imagination.

Now we will turn to the social and cultural atmosphere of the 1950s and 1960s—the era the Class of 1968 grew up in. These were turbulent times.

THE TURBULENT 1950S AND '60S

★ ★ ★

"Across the nation, campus unrest was growing, now with special emphasis on opposition to the draft. Large demonstrations were held in New York City and San Francisco. This was closely watched by VMI cadets and writers for The VMI CADET."
—VMI Superintendent General J. H. Binford Peay, III, April 2018, fiftieth class reunion

The Class of '68 was born in 1945-1946 and grew up during turbulent times in the US. They were the first of the post-World War II baby boomers. They grew up witnessing the end of the Jim Crow era of racial segregation, the struggle for civil rights, the growth of the middle class, the dawning of the environmental movement, nationwide protests over the war in Vietnam, and cultural rebellion among youth.

The year the Class of '68 graduated was not just any year in American history; it was a momentous year, and thus, no doubt, had a lasting influence on their lives. VMI Superintendent General J. H. Binford Peay III said, in his opening remarks at a dinner honoring the fiftieth reunion of the Class of 1968,

> ... it was an extraordinary time. *TIME* magazine described it as: "War Abroad, Riots at Home, Fallen Leaders, and Lunar

Dreams: The Year that Changed the World." It was a turning point not only in American history but across the globe. Countless books and studies have been written about the year 1968, and I believe historians will continue to focus on this period for decades to come.[80]

The January–February 2018 issue of *Smithsonian Magazine* was headlined "1968: The Year that Shattered America." The magazine called it a "seismic year." "Movements that had been building along the primary fault lines of the 1960s—the Vietnam War, the Cold War, civil rights, human rights, youth culture—exploded with force in 1968. The aftershocks registered both in America and abroad for decades afterward."[81]

VIETNAM WAR

First was the war in Vietnam, which began in 1955 when the United States sent military advisers to South Vietnam to assist in resisting the spread of communism from North Vietnam. The Vietnamese struggle to win independence from the French ended in 1954, with the partition of the country into the Western-backed South Vietnam and the Communist North Vietnam. The North Vietnamese, led by Ho Chi Minh, then tried to reunite Vietnam, but the South Vietnamese, backed by Americans, fiercely resisted this.

Initially, US participation was small. However, American involvement in Vietnam took a sharp turn in 1965 when the US government sent 3,500 troops into the war, the first of a wave of tens of thousands of troops that eventually landed there. By 1968, the number of American troops had increased to the point that the United States found itself embroiled in a bloody war. Public opinion in the United States and around the world increasingly opposed America's intervention in the war. The Vietnam War was the first major conflict to be fully televised, and people witnessed the horrors of the war every night in their living rooms. As a result, the protest movement against the war grew to be one of the largest ever seen in the United States and around the world.[82] People protested the methods used in fighting the war (napalm bombings and massacres) and the high loss of life. Conscripts burned their draft cards, and drafted young men fled to Canada.

The war ramped up in 1968. North Vietnam launched the Tet Offensive, a coordinated series of North Vietnamese attacks on over 100 cities and other targets in South Vietnam. The purpose was to stimulate rebellion among the South Vietnamese population and force back US involvement in the war. US and South Vietnamese forces held off the attacks, but the news coverage of the offensive shocked the American public, and support for the war further eroded. In a single week, in February 1968, more than 500 US troops were killed, and more than 2,500 were injured. This marked a turning point in the Vietnam War and the beginning of a slow and painful American withdrawal from the region.[83] That same year, protests against the Vietnam War exploded all across the United States, with some cities staging street protests every single day until the government pulled out US troops in 1973. By that time, 55,220 American troops had lost their lives in a war the United States never declared.

More than 3,800 men from VMI served in the war, and 42 lost their lives. None of those killed were from the Class of 1968.[84] When the Class of '68 matriculated at VMI, the Vietnam War was on every cadet's mind. How could it not be? These young men were preparing to be military officers, and there was little doubt that many of the 368 would be called into service. The draft was in force, and unless a cadet had a physical deferment, he would serve in some military capacity. Though none died, many from the Class of '68 who fought in the conflict still carry physical and mental scars from that war.

In the wider world, significant cultural changes were taking place. Not only were anti-war protests taking place on a nearly daily basis, but musicians and songwriters were getting involved in raising awareness about the horrors and futility of war and pleading for peace. The anti-war movement began to blend with the racial protests and the women's movement, and suddenly, the culture seemed to turn upside down. One of the big changes was the rising popularity of the British rock band the Beatles and their ultimate influence on public opinion around the Vietnam War.

In February 1964, with their songs already at the top of the charts, the Beatles arrived in the United States to play on the *Ed Sullivan Show*, one of the most popular variety shows on TV. Seventy-seven million Americans tuned in to watch them. Teenagers across the country and around the world went crazy for their music, and they became one of the most famous rock bands in the world. I remember that day vividly, myself a teenager, watching on a black-and-white TV—four talented young British men singing songs that seemed electric and my jumping around the room with excitement. A VMI cadet was in that room with me, the one I eventually married. I would bet that almost every cadet who entered VMI that year was a Beatles fan. But it does not end there. The Beatles had an impact on the anti-war movement in America, and in this way, Britain may have contributed to the eventual US pullout from Vietnam.

Influenced by Bertrand Russell, a well-known British anti-war activist and philosopher, the Beatles wrote several anti-war songs.[85] Paul McCartney had sought out Russell in the early 1960s and then spoke with John Lennon about the anti-war movement and what he had learned from Russell. In a 2008 interview, McCartney admitted that he hadn't known much about the war or paid much attention to it in the sixties. But after his meeting with Russell and his awakening, the Beatles' songs began to change. Their first anti-war song, "Revolution," came out in 1968.

Russell died in 1970, at ninety-seven, still protesting the war, and that same year, the Beatles broke up. John Lennon, still fiery over the Vietnam War, produced a stream of solo protest songs, including "Give Peace a Chance" and "Happy Xmas (War Is Over)." In 1971, he released "Imagine," his biggest hit and one still popular today, with the lyrics "Imagine all the people, livin' life in peace. . . . You may say I'm a dreamer, but I'm not the only one. I hope someday you'll join us, and the world will be as one."

To protest the war in Vietnam, Montana Congresswoman Jeannette Rankin led 5,000 women on a march in Washington, DC, on January 15, 1968. Their motto—"Sisterhood Is Powerful"—was picked up by the growing women's movement in the United States.

Also, in that same year, the movement toward meditation and Eastern mysticism, mostly out of California, began to grow slowly. In January 1968, the Beatles traveled to India to study Transcendental Meditation under the Maharishi Mahesh Yogi in Rishikesh, a city set in the foothills of the Himalayas in northern India. Apparently, the inspiration went both ways; even today, you can see murals of the Beatles and titles of their songs adorning the walls of the ashram. Because everything the Beatles did got attention in those days, their trip to India to study meditation and ways toward peace in the world was seen as a counterpoint to the Vietnam War and all wars—past, present, and future. Other famous singers and stars, such as the actress Mia Farrow and Mike Love of the Beach Boys, attended the same course. The consciousness of America and the world was shifting. People were questioning more than ever whether war was the way to achieve political ends.

CIVIL RIGHTS MOVEMENT

While war protests were building steam, the Civil Rights Movement had also been gaining strength since the early 1950s. In 1951, just down the road from Lexington and VMI, Barbara Johns, a sixteen-year-old Moton High School student in Farmville, Virginia, led a student strike over unequal high school conditions between the White and Black high schools. The White high school, Farmville High, had an industrial arts shop, locker rooms, an infirmary, a cafeteria, and a real auditorium, complete with sound equipment. The Black school, Moton High, was a brick building without the same amenities as the Farmville High school, but even more upsetting to Johns was that the school district had built tar paper shacks to house overflow students—shacks with potbelly stoves for heating and leaking roofs—two years earlier. The Moton High School Parent-Teacher Association had been lobbying the all-White school board for years to allocate money to build a new high school for Black children—which had become seriously overcrowded.

In October 1950, Johns, who lived fifteen miles from Farmville, missed the school bus for Black children when she ran home to retrieve her forgotten lunch. An hour later, she saw the school bus for White children approaching—knowing it would pass by the Moton High School—but it would not stop to let her ride. She said that was her deciding moment; unequal treatment of high school students had to end. In May 1951, Johns and other students held a two-week student strike that eventually led to the famous lawsuit *Brown v. Board of Education of Topeka*. (The case against the school board of Prince Edward County was joined with four other similar cases from Kansas, South Carolina, Delaware, and Washington, DC). Due to death threats against Barbara, her parents sent her to live with an uncle in Montgomery, Alabama, to complete her senior year of high school. [86]

In 1954, the Supreme Court settled *Brown v. Board of Education of Topeka*, ruling that maintaining segregation in separate but equal schools was unconstitutional and requiring that school districts across the country integrate their schools "with all deliberate speed." It was simply a fact that schools for Black children were underfunded and unequal to the schools for White children nearly across America. The resistance to integration among Whites was so fierce that it caused a tremendous social upheaval. White families pulled their children out of public schools (this happened in my family), and other White families moved to school districts where there were fewer Black children. White parents tried to physically block Black children from entering formerly all-White schools. I remember seeing on television, in the late 1950s, when I was still a child, White children and adults spitting on Black children in various parts of the South as they tried to enter public schools and feeling shocked by such behavior.

Even after the Supreme Court decision, the state of Virginia remained one of the most segregated states in the Union. In response to Brown v. Board of Education, the Prince Edward County School Board closed all the public schools from 1959 to 1964 rather than integrate Black and White students, during which time private schools were set up for White students. Black students studied in makeshift classrooms in churches or went to other parts of Virginia or other states to continue their schooling—or did not attend school at all for five years. Closing an entire public school system was so unusual that Attorney General Robert F. Kennedy said in a speech in Louisville, Kentucky, on March 18, 1963, that "The only places on earth not to provide free public education are Communist China, North Vietnam, Sarawak, Singapore, British Honduras—and Prince Edward County, Virginia." The impact on Black children in Prince Edward County had lasting effects on their lives.[87, 88]

In the fall of 1964, when I matriculated at Longwood College, Prince Edward County reopened its public schools. The entire five-year drama of the nearby county had made national headlines.[89] The 1964 VMI rats—the Class of '68—must have been aware of this drama.

In 1964 popular musician Bob Dylan came out with his hit, "The Times, They Are A- Changin." Yet there was much more change to come.

JONATHAN DANIELS

During this same period, one of VMI's graduates, Jonathan Daniels '61, was also part of the national struggle over civil rights. In the summer of 1965, Daniels, at the time a graduate divinity student from New England on a mission to support voting rights in Alabama, was shot by an off-duty deputy sheriff outside a small store in Loudoun County, Alabama while shielding a teenage girl named Ruby Sales.

Daniels had been arrested, along with several others, for volunteering to register African American citizens to vote. The group had just been released from a week in jail and simply entered a small store to buy soft drinks. The murder shocked the nation. The Class of '68 reacted in two ways—some mourning the loss of this fine man and others saying he got what he deserved. This was representative of the division of the South at the time, with some supporting civil rights and others resentful of Northern White people, like Daniels from New Hampshire, coming south to register Black voters, thereby disrupting the status quo of White supremacy at the ballot box.

THE CIVIL RIGHTS ACT

In 1964, President Lyndon B. Johnson signed the Civil Rights Act, one of the most important pieces of legislation in our nation's history. It ended segregation in public places and banned employment discrimination based on race, color, religion, sex, or national origin. Civil rights proponents considered it one of the crowning legislative achievements of the Civil Rights Movement. Next, President Johnson signed the Voting Rights Act of 1965. The act removed obstacles to voting, found mostly in Southern states, such as poll taxes and reading tests, that were intended to discourage African Americans from voting. In 1967, Johnson commissioned a study of the causes of the race riots that had become all too common across America, especially since 1960. The Kerner Commission report, released in February 1968, stated that the nation was "moving toward two societies, one black, one white—separate and unequal."

On April 4, 1968, a white supremacist shot and killed Martin Luther King Jr., leader of the national Civil Rights Movement. Riots broke out in more than 100 US cities over the next week, resulting in 39 deaths, 2,600 injured, and 21,000 people arrested. Two months later, on June 4, 1968, Robert F. Kennedy was assassinated in Los Angeles after winning the California primary as the presidential candidate for the Democratic Party. Only five years earlier, his brother, US President John F. Kennedy, had also been assassinated.

In August 1968, TV viewers of the Democratic National Convention in Chicago witnessed, live on television, police and National Guardsmen running amok, clubbing and tear-gassing hundreds of anti-war demonstrators and bystanders. Vice President Hubert Humphrey had won the nomination for president in a process clearly controlled by party bosses. Feeling the political system was rigged, demonstrators were using their rights—freedom of assembly and speech—to protest the decision, but to see this on television for the first time was shocking to the American public.

OTHER "FIRSTS" IN 1968

The year 1968 was seismic in other ways, too. That was the year President Johnson signed the Treaty on the Non-Proliferation of Nuclear Weapons, the primary means of preventing the spread of nuclear weapons to nonnuclear states.

All the while, protests in various forms against the Vietnam War were occurring weekly across the nation. A day did not go by without some shocking new images of war, protests, civil rights abuses, or racially motivated murders. We thought our country was falling apart.

By 1968, the contraceptive pill had taken hold in America, throwing the Catholic Church into a theological crisis. Struggling with the concept of preventing potential souls from being born, Pope Paul VI, in July 1968, issued *Humanae Vitae* (human life), reaffirming the Church's opposition to artificial contraception. This was bucking a strong upward trend in women's rights to control their own bodies and determine the number of children they wanted to bear. Women saw "the pill" as their release from the bondage of willy-nilly childbearing, making it possible for them to both marry and achieve their educational and career dreams. Many religious people feared it would result in a "sexual revolution" that would encourage sex outside of marriage, with the fear of pregnancy alleviated.

Yet the sexual revolution had already started before "the pill" was invented. Since at least the beginning of the decade, a push to legalize abortion advanced, with formidable opposition from the John Birch Society and others. The result was much more open talk about sex in American society. The turmoil over contraception and abortion was occurring while *Playboy* magazine and other pornographic magazines were reaching their heyday, urging men to do whatever they wanted without regard to the consequences.

In another first, Black athlete Arthur Ashe from Richmond, Virginia, won the US Open, the first Black man to win a Grand Slam tennis tournament. That same year, Yale University decided to admit female students, beginning in 1969, and Virginia Military Institute decided to admit Black male cadets, beginning in the fall of 1968.

Paradoxically, the cadets at VMI during these tumultuous times were largely shielded from events occurring in the outer world due to lack of access to television (except at the post PX), and their days were filled with rigorous physical and military training and full-schedule academic courses. But more importantly, cadets had little free time outside their military and academic life. They rarely left post for any length of time, so they had little opportunity to discuss current events with family or friends. Many commented that they existed in a bubble, surviving the rigors and demands of their military and physical training and academics. "We would only find out what was happening in the world when we went home for holidays and during summer break," one graduate wrote.

PHOTOS

★ ★ ★

CLASS OF '68

Figure 1 Five rat roommates in fatigues, 1964. Bob Crenshaw, Paul Hebert, Victor Huang, Walt Jeffries, Rick Siegel. "We all looked like criminals" - Creigh Kelley.

Figure 2 Author and Paul Hebert 1964

Figure 3 Class of 1968 cadets in barracks: Walt Jeffries, Rick Siegel, Paul Hebert, Bob Schmalzriedt, Victor Huang, Chuck Maddox and Jim Burg.

Figure 4 Author and Paul Hebert at Ring Figure Ball, 1966.

Figure 5 Class of 1968 at 50th Reunion.

CADETS TODAY

Figure 1 Cadets in 2019 marching penalty tours

Figure 2 Cadets 'at ease' 2019

Figure 3 Female cadet 2023

VMI MEMORIAL STATUES AND PLAQUES

Figure 1 Confederate General Thomas 'Stonewall' Jackson statue at head of VMI parade ground, erected in 1912 and removed in 2020.

Figure 2 Plaque honoring Jonathan M. Daniels.

Figure 3 Entrance to Daniels Courtyard created in 2005.

Figure 4 General George Washington statue erected 1856.

Figure 5 Virginia Mourning Her Dead statue commemorating cadets who died at the Battle of New Market. Photo courtesy of VMI Archives.

Figure 6 Memorial Hall, formerly named Jackson Memorial Hall, 1916, with 1914 Battle of New Market painting by Clinedinst.

THE 1960S—A VMI TURNING POINT

★ ★ ★

"In February 1968, it was reported that VMI had accepted its first Black cadet and that four others were also being evaluated for admission. The next year, 1968-69, would see the first Black cadets enrolled at VMI. The admission of women, however, would wait for another thirty years."
—VMI Superintendent General J. H. Binford Peay III,
April 2018, fiftieth class reunion

In 1967, VMI began moving into a new era of inclusiveness. VMI Superintendent George R. E. Shell announced to the VMI BOV that the Institute would admit Black students into the Class of '72, with admission beginning in the fall of 1968. According to the *VMI Alumni Review*, there was no further discussion or debate.[90]

BLACK MALE CADETS

The admission of five Black male cadets in the fall of 1968 signaled a momentous turning point for VMI. The US Military Academy at West Point had admitted its first Black cadet in 1870 and had its first Black graduate in 1877. But West Point admitted very few Black cadets. A second African American cadet graduated ten years later in 1887, and the third thirty-five years later in 1922. Why it took so long for VMI and the other well-known military college in South

Carolina, The Citadel, to racially integrate is easy to infer. Racism and racial segregation in the South were too deep and stubborn. Nearly all Virginia colleges were racially segregated in the 1960s.

These Black cadets who matriculated at VMI in the fall of 1968 saw the Institute with different eyes and began to change it. Even from the first months of that 1968-1969 academic year, Black cadets were raising awareness about inappropriate customs and traditions that earlier White cadets would have never questioned. Some refused to salute the Confederate flag flown at ball games, ceremonies, and parades. One, who played drums, stopped drumming when the band played "Dixie." They refused to salute the Jackson statue, a requirement when exiting barracks through the Jackson Arch, or the Lee Chapel on the campus of Washington & Lee University when walking by.§§§ They took guard duty to avoid participating in VMI Confederate ceremonies, such as New Market Day. Their quiet protests sparked debate on post over the existence of Confederate symbolism, and they helped lead to the elimination of some of it.

In 1973, Black students, whose numbers had grown, threatened to go AWOL for the New Market Ceremony. In response, the entire Corps of Cadets voted, and it was decided, narrowly, to eliminate the playing of "Dixie" and the display of the Confederate flag at the ceremony. The VMI BOV, not happy with this development, voted to change nothing in the ceremony, but the Institute nonetheless dropped the playing of "Dixie" and held New Market Day after graduation, making attendance voluntary. By the late 1970s, VMI had completely abandoned the Confederate flag, and saluting the Lee Chapel became voluntary. First-year cadets, however, were still required to salute the Jackson statue.[91] VMI was evolving.

DANIELS MEMORIAL

It took another twenty years for the next big values shift to take

---

§§§ Lee is buried in a sarcophagus in what was formerly called the Lee Chapel on the campus of Washington and Lee University. In 2021, the university renamed it University Chapel.

place at VMI. The murder of Jonathan Daniels in 1965 was slowly settling into a broader context. In 1998, the VMI BOV established the Jonathan Daniels Humanitarian Award to honor the ultimate sacrifice of this graduate.¶¶¶ The five recipients to date have been President Jimmy Carter in 2001; Ambassador Andrew Young in 2006; Dr. Paul Hebert, Class of 1968, in 2011; US Congressman John Lewis in 2015; and Carolyn Miles of Save the Children in 2019. VMI gave small bronze replicas of *Virginia Mourning Her Dead* to the first three recipients of the award. In 2015, VMI changed the design of the award to a shaped etched-glass figure. How might John Lewis have felt about receiving a replica of a monument to the Civil War? Clearly, someone at VMI had posed that question!

In addition to the award, in 2006, the Institute built the Daniels Memorial Plaza, a place for quiet contemplation. Situated right behind the Old Barracks, the courtyard contains a stone relief of Daniels and a plaque honoring the recipients of the award in his name so all incoming cadets are made aware of the sacrifice of this cadet. VMI commemorates Daniels's death every spring in the courtyard with Taps and a brief memorial speech. The recognition of Jonathan Daniels's sacrifice—in the pursuit of civil rights for all—represented a spiritual shift for VMI.

A SECOND PERIOD OF MEMORIALS TO ALUMNI—2009

Respect for the greatness of George C. Marshall's influence on peace and stability in the twentieth century continued to grow nationally and internationally. In 2009, VMI completed the construction of the George C. Marshall Hall. Within its walls are the Center for

---

¶¶¶ The Promaji Club, a club of African American cadets, created the Jonathan Daniels Humanitarian Award and gave it to Cabell Brand in 1992. Brand was a 1944 graduate of VMI, humanitarian, and philanthropist. The VMI BOV made the award an official VMI award in 1998.

Leadership and Ethics and the VMI Hall of Valor—scores of framed medals VMI graduates have earned in times of war. In front of Marshall Hall is a memorial garden dedicated to Marshall, with a quote by Marshall inscribed on a concrete wall:

> IT IS TO YOU MEN AND WOMEN OF THIS GREAT CITIZEN-ARMY WHO CARRIED THIS NATION TO VICTORY THAT WE MUST LOOK FOR LEADERSHIP IN THE CRITICAL YEARS AHEAD. YOU ARE YOUNG AND VIGOROUS AND YOUR SERVICES AS INFORMED CITIZENS WILL BE NECESSARY TO THE PEACE AND PROSPERITY OF THE WORLD.
> 26 NOVEMBER 1945

The creation of the Daniels award, courtyard, and solemn annual ceremony was way off in the future when the Class of '68 arrived on post. In 1965, attitudes toward Daniels's death were different. He was a Northerner protesting Black voter suppression at a time when discrimination against Black people was so severe that they could not exercise the basic rights of American citizenship. Jim Crow laws—separating Black and White people into a caste system that prevented African Americans from entering restaurants and hotels intended for White people or attending an institution, such as VMI—were still practiced throughout the South. Southern people accepted this as the norm, and thus, Daniels's actions in Alabama to register Black citizens to vote defied Southern customs and reason. Some VMI cadets in that era were not sympathetic to his death, and it took VMI more than thirty years to recognize his greatness.

Thus, when they arrived on campus, the Class of 1968 beheld a post memorializing President George Washington, General Thomas "Stonewall" Jackson, former Superintendents Smith and Cocke, and George C. Marshall. These memorials to great men continued to provide visible support to the code of honor, but VMI had not yet addressed or faced the call to integration. It had not yet admitted any students with an African American heritage. And although the women's movement had already begun in the 1960s, VMI viewed the admission of women as unthinkable. Yet, twenty-nine years later, VMI was admitting women.

FEMALE CADETS ADMITTED

In the spring of 2019, I taught a course at VMI in biological anthropology. In my class of ten students was an African American woman named Ariana Ruffin. She told me that her uncle had researched her family history and found that she was a descendant of people enslaved by the same Edmund Ruffin who joined the VMI cadets at the execution of John Brown in 1856 in Charles Town, West Virginia. Yet, she admitted to knowing little about Edmund Ruffin and his ties to VMI.

Edmund Ruffin, who could not bear to live knowing Virginia would have to let go of slavery when the South lost the war, could not have imagined a descendant of his own slaves—and a female, at that—ever becoming a VMI cadet. And yet, Cadet Ruffin attending my class is a living testimony to the remarkable changes that have taken place at VMI, in Virginia, and in the nation in the last 180 years.

The admission of female cadets to VMI, in August 1997, was far more momentous than the admission of African American males had been; there was much more resistance to admitting women, and it came about only because of a Supreme Court decision. One graduate of the Class of '68 referred to this period of arguments against admitting women as "an embarrassing chapter in VMI history." Many VMI alumni thought the Institute would be ruined with the admission of females, even though the United States Military Academy at West Point had successfully admitted females in 1976, following an act of Congress[92], a full twenty-one years of positive experience. They argued that if state-supported schools must admit women, VMI should break its ties with the state of Virginia and become a private college.

The decision to admit women and maintain a state-supported college passed the BOV by only one vote. Cadet Ruffin exemplifies how VMI has, in fact, survived and thrived with the changes in the gender and racial makeup of its student body. In 2019, VMI had 1,726 students—6 percent Black cadets (comparable to the University of Virginia) and 14 percent female cadets (compared to 20 percent at West Point).

I asked Cadet Ruffin why she wanted to attend VMI. She said that she simply wanted a career in the military. She was born and raised in Philadelphia, attended Catholic girls' schools, and is at VMI on a track and field scholarship. For her, slavery, the Civil War, and Edmund Ruffin seem light-years in the past and no longer relevant to her life.

While VMI, in the past fifty years, has sought to move out of a Civil War persona and into the modern age, the town of Lexington still sends Confederate signals. Ty Seidule, historian and professor emeritus of history at West Point, writes in his memoir *Robert E. Lee and Me - A Southerner's Reckoning with the Myth of the Lost Cause*,[93] "Today, as a historian, when I walk the streets of Lexington, I see evidence of the Lost Cause Myth. The late Tony Horwitz, the author of the brilliant book *Confederates in the Attic*, called Lexington 'the second city of Confederate remembrance: Medina to Richmond's Mecca.'"[94]

Indeed, several prominent Confederate leaders and officers are buried in the Jackson Cemetery in downtown Lexington. The largest grave monument is that of Stonewall Jackson. Other historical markers in Lexington are the Jackson House and the Chapel dedicated to Robert E. Lee on the Washington and Lee University campus. These burials and buildings serve as Lexington's tourist draw.

AN INEVITABLE RECKONING

In 2017, VMI came under scrutiny following a serious incident in Charlottesville, Virginia, where White supremacists marched to prevent the city from removing a statue of Robert E. Lee. Following the murder of George Floyd in Minneapolis in May 2020, there were renewed calls across the nation to remove Confederate statues. After the Charlottesville incident, Governor Northam, a 1981 VMI graduate, decided that Virginia needed to rebuke racism in all forms in the state. He encouraged localities to take down their Confederate statues and remove other related symbols. Owing to a controversy of whether to remove the Jackson statue at VMI, on October 26, 2020, General Peay submitted his resignation.

On October 29, 2020, the VMI BOV voted to have the Jackson statue removed from post and relocated to the New Market Battlefield State Park in New Market, Virginia. It was a transformative decision. The Jackson statue had served as a VMI focal point for 108 years. Its removal represented an end to a tradition and ideology. These changes were painful for so many alumni, including the resignation of General Peay, who had served admirably for the past eighteen years as superintendent. Soon after, the BOV selected retired Major General Cedric T. Wins, VMI Class of 1985, to serve as interim superintendent while a search committee looked for General Peay's successor. The BOV selected Major General Wins, and he now serves as VMI's first African American superintendent.

In mid-October 2020, Governor Northam called for a third-party review of the Institute's "culture, policies, practices and equity in disciplinary procedures" regarding the treatment of Black cadets on post, completed in spring of 2021. VMI is tasked with the implementation of recommendations from the review.[95] An important observation that came from the review was that the Honor Code and Honor System at VMI should be maintained, and it constitutes one of the strongest and most positive features of the Institute.

A THEME OF HONOR THROUGH LIFE

★ ★ ★

"It may seem trite, but these values hold true. They are necessary for a successful career, marriage, and life."
—A graduate, Class of '68

The VMI Class of '68 matriculated in 1964, exactly 99 years after the end of the Civil War, and the leveling of VMI by Union forces. This was fifty-two years after the erection of the Stonewall Jackson statue and thirty-three years after the erection of the General Francis Smith statue. But these Confederate symbols seemed to have little impact on these cadets. This is because, by 1964, the focus had shifted away from these revered war heroes of the South to America's new hero, General George C. Marshall. That year, the George C. Marshall Museum and Library opened on post, and fifteen years earlier, an arch to "New Barracks" had been named for Marshall. Marshall stood for all that was good about the American military—winning a war against an evil enemy, the Marshall Plan to reconstruct Europe, and a Nobel Peace Prize in 1953. One graduate said that when he entered VMI, they looked to Marshall, not the Confederates, for their inspiration.

While many of the new cadets were born and raised in the South, they had also been born at the end of World War II, and the paradigm was shifting away from what looked to them like ancient history and toward American patriotism and feeling like they lived in the greatest country in the world. Some cadets were disturbed by American involvement in Vietnam, feeling like we should not be engaged in that war, but overall, they were not focused on the Confederacy. And while one could still hear shouts at football games—"save your Dixie cups, the South will rise again"—it was all joking. They might sing "Dixie" and wave a Confederate flag, but it was mostly in fun, for they knew it was over—way over. The Confederate statues and other symbols and rituals were still there, but whose agenda was that? Nobody dared suggest their removal or elimination because these were regarded as VMI's "history." In fact, they had been important in the past, but now, for these cadets of the 1960s, it was military life, preparing them to become officers in a US branch of the military, and the VMI Honor System that guided their lives.

One graduate says that VMI takes ordinary high school graduates and turns most of them into extraordinary men. The accomplishments of this class show this, but it also shows that most of those extraordinary men had most of the same joys, trials, and tragedies as the rest of us. They married, had children and grandchildren, experienced divorces, lost loved ones, and had mental health challenges, much like the rest of the American population.

After leaving VMI, over half of the Class of '68 stayed exclusively in the United States, but only 8 percent spent the rest of their working lives in Virginia. The others lived both in the US and abroad during their careers: Vietnam, Germany, Korea, and other countries in Europe and Asia. Most of these locations were related to their military service. Today, three-quarters of the men live in Virginia and other Southern states, and the remaining quarter live in the Northeast, West, and Southwest.

MILITARY SERVICE

In 1968, VMI graduates were required to take commissions in their chosen branch of service, unless they had a physical exemption or educational deferment. Among those surveyed, 90 percent did serve, while the remaining 10 percent may have received medical deferments. Over 50 percent served one to five years. Another 36 percent served six to thirty years, and two men served more than thirty years. Nearly three-quarters of these men served in the Army soon after leaving VMI, and nearly a quarter served in the Air Force. Five served in the Marines, and two in the Navy. About half of the men experienced combat, and nearly all of those fought in Vietnam. Of the majority who served one to five years, over half were ranked as lieutenants and captains. A third were majors, lieutenant colonels, and colonels, closely aligned with the 36 percent who served six to thirty years. One graduate in the VMI Class of '68 became a general. General Peay's office determined that 15 graduates had careers in a branch of the military, serving 20 years or more.

The men said that their military service taught them that the military succeeds because it teaches leadership, organization, management, and teamwork. Everyone needs to cooperate and follow the rules. You need to respect your commanding officer (CO) even if you do not like him. They carried these lessons into their careers, which helped them lead organizations and build successful professional lives.

Another common theme was that people are always asked to lead at some point in their lives, and they may not be ready for it. Many respondents said that they were successful with leadership opportunities because of their experience at VMI and through military service.

Many said that their military service taught them that life is precious and fragile, that every day and every friend is to be treasured. For example, one man said, "Most of what we consider to be life's difficulties and entanglements are simply not important when compared with the realities of possibly being killed at any moment, as in war."

Most emphasized that they had learned at VMI and in the military to stay principled and always do the right thing. They said that integrity, honesty, honor, discipline, and loyalty are not just words—but words to live by each day. One man expressed,

I wouldn't say I learned them from the military, but VMI and my military service certainly reinforced the fundamental principles and life lessons I was taught by my parents and family. Those being: to be God-fearing, honest, humble, and always responsible for your decisions, actions, and conduct. Further, that the greatest responsibility in my life, should I decide to become a husband and father, is to do all I can to be sure my children are God-fearing, honest, responsible adults.

Another life principle frequently mentioned was taking responsibility for actions. When things go wrong, don't try to blame others. Several said things like "Do not just speak your values; live by them and show others that you walk the talk." Several said they learned that the citizen-soldier is the bedrock of our country. Service to country is what keeps our country strong. Serving in the military gives you that sense that you have done what is right.

Many remarked that there was not much diversity at VMI or in their high schools or communities and that the military was the first place they learned about cultural and ideological diversity. This taught them that all of us need to learn to appreciate people who think differently and learn from them. Even if people are different and we do not agree with their point of view, we should always show respect for those we command.

CAREERS

Most of the men who participated in the survey did not pursue military careers and went on to mostly professional positions in business, engineering, teaching, public service, or law. Eight practiced medicine, and three went into the clergy. A few men changed careers, moving from engineering to public service or from law or medicine to teaching. Ten men eventually worked in internet technology and communications, a field that developed at least two decades after they left VMI. An astonishing 98 percent of the men said they were happy with their chosen profession, and nearly all said that VMI had prepared them well for their professions.

When asked about the life lessons they learned from their nonmilitary careers, many replied that these were the same as lessons learned from military service, especially the principles underpinning right living. However, work offered many additional lessons. They said it is essential to display integrity in everything we do. In business, integrity and honesty are the most important elements of professional success. "Without integrity, personal relationships fail, families fail, businesses fail, governments can fail, societies can fail." And "If the VMI Honor Code were universally accepted, our country and the world would be much better." Further, "In all circumstances, be considerate of others."

Several men stated that no one is perfect, no organization is perfect, and we will make mistakes. The most important takeaway is that we learn from our mistakes. Mistakes are great teachers. "Mistakes and accidents are inevitable, so they must be anticipated, kept to a minimum, analyzed, corrected, and learned from to optimize prevention and response."

Other lessons the men imparted read like a book about how to be a good person. They emphasized being open, trustworthy, empathetic, and tolerant. "How important it is to treat every individual with respect!" "Treating people fairly and consistently leads to good results and high morale." And "At their core, people around the world are much the same. Hard work, relationships, and business courage are required for success." Others said it is important to give credit to others for achievements. "Play fair. Share the credit—or better, I give it to one of my staff. Praise in public, punish in private." And "Give credit publicly to those who enabled successful projects/outcomes."

The men emphasized finding a profession we enjoy. They wrote: "Find what you enjoy doing and do it. I have been very well compensated, but I did not 'work' for a living." And "Follow your heart, and don't be afraid to march to the beat of a different drummer

(Thoreau) or take the road less traveled (Frost)." "Follow your bliss. If you're not happy, make a change." "Find a job/career you love and stick with it."

Another important lesson they offered was living life with love. One person expressed, "You only go around once, and you try to do it right. Don't spend too much time trying to 'fix' others. Love of the Lord is key to all. You don't take anything with you when you leave this world. Love with all your being." And "Stay in touch with your good friends, and never ask them for anything, but always be there for them." "Try to live at peace with yourself and peace with others."

They affirmed how important it is to figure out priorities in life. Many emphasized that we should prioritize family above all and have a lifelong goal to live a life that attempts to put honor above self. In addition, one wrote, "Don't sweat the small stuff. . . . It's all small stuff. Life is short. . . . Eat dessert first. Save for the rainy days; they will come."

They maintained that relationships are the foundation of a successful career. "Most key decisions are made based upon relationships over merit. Work hard, do good work, but build strong enduring relationships." "Your success depends on how well you treat others."

They also said we need to learn how to make good decisions. "Test everything multiple times. Sleep on everything before making a decision. If you can't figure something out, analyze the crap out of it, then go do something else and then sleep on it, and in the morning, you'll figure it out." Avoid getting into the wrong businesses. For example, "Never get involved with a multilevel marketing company unless you want to lose all your friends and get frustrated and end up hating yourself. Or stated differently, avoid dream merchants."

Many said that if we want to be successful in business (or in any profession), we must be willing to lead and that VMI was a great teacher of leadership skills. Be "prepared and willing to take on difficult and new issues." We must also be hands-on leaders and managers. "You must know what your employees are doing and make sure that they have the tools to work and succeed." But most importantly, in a leadership position, we need "to respect, mentor, challenge, and support the advancement of those who work for you. Give opportunities to those under your charge. Maintain flexibility and a positive attitude. Do not tolerate dishonesty or harassment of any type."

One person offered specific advice on figuring out a retirement plan. "Start a Roth IRA as soon as you start working, and contribute something, anything, to it every month, until you quit working. This is on top of any retirement plan you have at your job."

MARRIAGE AND CHILDREN

All 121 men married, and twenty-four of them married their Ring Figure dates. A little over half married within two years of graduating from VMI, and nearly all were married by 1979. Today, nearly two-thirds of the Class of 1968 is still married to the same woman, having maintained a marriage for thirty-six to fifty years. A few were divorced along the way, and very few lost their spouses to death. Thirty-two men had married twice, ten had married three times, one had married four times, and one had married five times.

They said the keys to a successful marriage are love, commitment, shared values, similar goals and interests, the ability to apologize for wrongdoings, the ability to compromise, respect for each other, trust, friendship, tolerance, honesty, listening, and laughter. A few mentioned the importance of God in their marriages, and others mentioned the importance of children in solidifying their unions. But most emphasized this desire to make things work through honesty, trust, tolerance, respect, and compromise.

Those who divorced said their marriages lacked the very elements mentioned above, namely shared values and goals, an ability to compromise, selflessness, and honesty, and they had failed to address problems in their marriages with honesty. Some mentioned that one or both spouses were too immature to be married and that infidelity had led to a few divorces. Only one man mentioned financial difficulty as a cause for divorce. Like most Americans from this era, three-quarters of the men had two or three children.

When I asked the men what advice they would give to current and future cadets about marriage, they answered that it is important to finish education before getting married and having a family. One wrote, "It is vital to get as much education as possible before you start a family and a career. After you're involved in those things, there probably won't be time to continue your education while adequately meeting your other responsibilities." Others advised careful consideration. "Think long and hard before getting married, and take compatibility tests to make sure you two are actually compatible. There is no rush, so triple-check before getting hitched." Some also advised "seeking a balance between work and family."

The question that generated the most responses was about the lessons learned from marriage, whether it had lasted long or ended in divorce. They said that marriages can survive and thrive despite grave mistakes if we exercise understanding and maturity, are committed, have common goals, love our children, and extend forgiveness. Good communication is essential, and patience is required for long-term success. "There has to be give and take; real love grows over time." And "Don't take your spouse and marriage for granted." "It is easy to give up and hard to stay committed, but staying committed is very rewarding." "You have to maintain open communications about all aspects of your relationship and share interests with your partner." The men emphasized trust, respect, tolerance for human imperfections, keeping a sense of humor, communicating well, having common interests, and, most of all, forgiveness.

They also wrote wisdom of the ages for maintaining a strong marriage. "Cooperation is usually better than 'winning.' We try to remember daily why we got married, and we share that thought daily." "Marriage is about trust, understanding, and giving. If you have problems with sex, finances, in-laws, or religion, address these issues early, and do not expect them to correct themselves." "Show your love every day. Always share. Be a team and be best friends." Some said that uncontrolled anger can put a marriage in danger. "Never let anger shape what you say." Another wrote, "Something my father taught me that I had to relearn: Never go to bed angry." Others talked about the importance of listening as part of quality communication. "Communication is key to many situations. Winning an argument isn't that important. Try to be more interested in the mate's life interests. Spend more time at the end of the day one-on-one (probably the MOST important). I neglected this early on."

Some took a humorous tack: "My wife is always right." "The other person is one-hundred-percent right all the time. Give one hundred percent. Take zero percent. It's that easy." Men said to do whatever it takes to spend our lives with our partner, someone we love; it's worth it. "The whole is greater than the sum of its parts!"

If I could wrap up the valuable answers of these men into one box, it would be this: Express loving kindness throughout our lives. Put love above all, be kind and respectful to everyone, and live life according to the VMI Honor Code, and we will succeed in life. They said if everyone follows this code of conduct, the world will be a better place.

One '68 graduate who served in Vietnam and whose life reflects many of the themes expressed by the class is Creigh Kelley.

CREIGH KELLEY

★ ★ ★

CLASS OF '68, VIETNAM VETERAN

Ninety percent of the graduates of the Class of '68 served at least some time in the military. About half of them went to Vietnam. Creigh Kelley was one of those. But Creigh did not make the military his career. He was an athlete at heart, a runner. His feelings about VMI begin with hating it and then, after many years, loving it, appreciating it, and defending it.

Creigh was one of the few students in his class who grew up a "Yankee." Although accused of being a Yankee, Creigh had been raised with Southern lore and values. Born in Winchester, Virginia, Creigh's family moved several times before he was eight years old to New York, New Jersey, and Westport, Connecticut, on dairy and chicken farms that his father managed. Creigh had attended Staples High School in Westport and described himself as an average student, "but my running on the cross-country and track teams was interesting to a few colleges."

Creigh ended up at VMI primarily because his mother wanted him to go there. She had grown up in Clarke County, Virginia, had attended Sweet Briar College, and had gone to dances at VMI. She wanted him to go to a school in Virginia, even though he had been accepted to Bates College in Maine. He applied to William and Mary College, the University of Virginia, Washington & Lee, and VMI. As he applied late to these colleges, all except VMI had put him on a waitlist. He visited VMI in the spring during hop [dance] weekend, saw the new indoor track, and was escorted around by a couple of top VMI runners who told him he shouldn't worry about the Rat Line. "It was an easy choice over cold, snowy Maine."

AT VMI

"VMI was a cosmic shock to me when I arrived." Creigh said,

> It was nothing like what I had seen the previous spring. It was terrifying and horrible. I cried into my pillow the entire first week. I knew I was stuck because my parents would never forgive me if I left, plus my brother had flunked out of a junior college the year before, and my dad put him into the Army forty-eight hours later. I never forgot that. Interestingly, my brother survived three years in the Army and then went on to get his undergrad and graduate degrees in finance and became very successful. I disliked the confrontations in the Rat Line, where we were challenged on almost anything. A distinct memory was seared into my brain almost the first day. A cadre member asked me, "What was the coolest thing you did this year, Rat?" I replied, "Sir, I went to the *Ed Sullivan Show* and saw the Beatles!" He screamed at me, "You aren't allowed to lie, Rat!" I was stunned but stammered, "I'm not lying! I was there!" He dropped me for a huge number of

push-ups, and at that moment, I hated VMI.

I asked Creigh if he felt he was living in a "bubble" at VMI. "Absolutely." He replied,

> We envied the students at other colleges, with seemingly no restrictions and endless freedom. I was content to live day-to-day in my silo: cross-country, indoor track, and outdoor track. I was close to my teammates and tried to stay out of trouble. I only encountered the "real world" when I was home in the summer. I remember trying to explain what VMI was like to my former high school classmates and failing miserably. After our rat year, I felt an incredible relief.
>
> I was pleased with my performance in track my first year, and my teammates elected me as the honorary rat track captain. I was really surprised. Plus, I had to get an A on my rat chemistry exam to become a 3rd Class cadet (anything less would mean summer school), and I studied all night and pulled it off. Unfortunately, I was super lazy about studying and did just enough to get by. In retrospect, I could have done so much more.

Creigh said he was not troubled by the Stonewall Jackson statue or other Civil War symbols and rituals at VMI. "I knew that I had relatives that had fought on both sides," he said. He went on to explain his North/South upbringing:

> My father grew up in Connecticut, and we visited my maternal grandmother's home in Virginia every summer, so I liked the South. I revered General Lee and several of the more colorful leaders. My mother always reminded me that the correct term was "The War Between the States" and not the "Civil War." I was impressed by the Battle of

New Market. I felt proud of the traditions and never linked them intellectually to slavery. I knew that slavery had been abolished correctly and somehow reconciled that VMI probably used slaves. It has been only since the events of 2020 that I have rethought everything.

Despite the Vietnam War and the Civil Rights Movement being the top national issues of the day, Creigh said these topics were not much discussed when he was at VMI:

> Initially, the nonstop activities and pressure in every aspect of VMI consumed me. After our rat year, I returned in the fall of 1965, after a summer of Northern culture, where everyone was talking about Vietnam and civil rights. I recall how strange I thought VMI cadets were in their general disdain for Black people, whereas, in Connecticut, the Civil Rights Movement was a positive topic.
>
> The first couple of years, I don't recall any professors bringing up anything controversial. As an English major in the final two years, I remember Professor Greet and Colonel Dillard openly discussing difficult topics, including racism and suicide. They brought Willian Styron (1925-2006) in to discuss his first novel, *Lie Down in Darkness* (1951), a story of betrayals and infidelities in a Southern family. ****

I asked Creigh whether he had heard anything about the murder of Jonathan Daniels in the summer of 1965. He said he probably did, but "it is not a huge memory. Honestly, I'm not even sure the flag was at half-mast. If it was a topic, I missed the memo."

During his last two years at VMI, Creigh recalls that the Vietnam

---

****   After his VMI visit, Styron went on to write Pulitzer-prize-winning *The Confessions of Nat Turner* (1967) and the international best-seller *Sophie's Choice* (1979).

War became more of a central topic. "Many of us knew the clock was ticking. As I look back on the last two years, I think we viewed ourselves as patriots, and we were resolved to fight for our country. We were not supportive of the anti-war movement because it was essentially antithetical to VMI."

Dr. Martin Luther King Jr. was assassinated during Creigh's 1st Class year on April 4, 1968. "Most of us were shocked, and we discussed it, particularly in light of Black cadets arriving in the fall of 1968."

Creigh said he felt fine about the admission of Black cadets:

> I felt it was overdue. I grew up in a town with few Black people, but the vice president of my Staples High School senior class in Westport was Black. My parents were not overtly racist, but they made it clear that our family were better people. I never bought into it and confronted them periodically on that subject, especially when I was in high school.

In the fall of 1968, after graduation, Creigh had a new job as acting secretary of the VMI Foundation. Because the VMI administration regarded Creigh as a Yankee, they thought he could serve as a go-between with new Black students. Soon after the new class of rats arrived, the head of the foundation, Joe Neikirk, Class of 1932, told Creigh that Superintendent Shell wanted him to go over to the barracks, report to the commandant, who would assign one of his staff to escort him to the room of the five new Black cadets and visit with them. Neikirk said, "Make them understand what it's going to be like." Creigh asked, "Why me, sir?" Neikirk answered, "Because you're from the North and can communicate better with them." Creigh continued, "I made the trek over and spoke with them for maybe thirty minutes. They were as overwhelmed as I had been as a rat. I gave them an unvarnished appraisal of how tough it would be for them. After that, I never spoke to any of them again. It was a bit surreal."

Creigh laughed at the story. Clearly, he said, the administration had no idea how to welcome the new Black cadets.

AFTER VMI

In April 1969, Creigh received orders to go to Vietnam in the fall. Beth, his fiancée, moved up their wedding date to May 1969, and in September, they headed down to Fort Sill, Oklahoma, where Creigh began a three-month training to become a basic artillery officer. They then moved to Fort Gordon, Georgia, for training to be a civil affairs officer, pushing his date for deployment to Vietnam to December 1969. Arriving in Vietnam on December 18, Creigh was assigned to an airmobile 155 artillery battery. They moved around for about six months, including the invasion of Cambodia. Soon after, Creigh was made first lieutenant and volunteered to be a liaison officer with a regional force and popular force company (roughly like the US National Guard) known as the "Ruff Puffs." He served with them for the remaining six months of his tour of duty. "It was exciting," Creigh said,

> ... because I had a couple or three enlisted team members, and we were living in a bunker on an outpost with 100 Vietnamese troops and families. I had no officer to report to other than the Vietnamese captain. My role was to go out on operations with these troops and call in US artillery to support their combat operations. A few weeks later, a chopper landed, and a small new team of US infantry troops showed up. The first lieutenant, with his three enlisted people, was Dee Biggs, Class of '68, with whom I had run track and cross-country all four years at VMI!

A few months later, the Army ordered Creigh to another small post just off the South China Sea to support another Vietnamese unit. He worked with them until a week before leaving Vietnam. "I did one crazy thing while there." Creigh relayed,

The intel said the area was calm, with no evidence of major enemy units. So, I grabbed an old pair of jungle boots, nailed each of them to a slat of ammo box wood, grabbed a long rope, and asked my team if they wanted to go with me to the nearby beach and try to water ski. "Of course!" they replied. I said, "Grab an extra machine gun, and we'll let one guy drive the jeep, one guy will ski, and one guy will set up a firing position to cover us." And we did! It was crazy and a blast, and we got away with it! That night, another unit got into a major firefight in the jungle bluffs above that beach. A North Vietnamese Army battalion had secretly infiltrated the area and was likely watching the stupid Americans on the beach.

Creigh was glad to leave Vietnam the week before Christmas 1970. Before he left, he was on a final operation in the jungle when he received a radio call at about 2 a.m. from his battalion commander, a person he had never met, who told him he wasn't supposed to have volunteered to go on the final operation. That meant he was now a few hundred miles from where he was supposed to be. His commander sent a CIA pilot to collect him as he walked out of the jungle. The pilot loaded him into a fixed-wing unmarked two-seater airplane and flew him back to the battalion base. Creigh then flew to Japan and then Seattle, where he called Beth after battling through an anti-war demonstration at the gate to reach a public phone. It was a disappointing return to America.

From Seattle, Creigh took a flight to Washington, DC, and needed to call Beth to pick him up at the airport. But he didn't have any cash or coins to make the phone call. "I dialed the operator, told her I needed to reverse the charges, explaining the situation, and she put the call through for free. That sort of made up for the struggle through the demonstration at the Seattle Airport!"

But then there was another disconcerting incident:

Waiting for her to pick me up early that morning, an Army major approached me and informed me that I was out of uniform. I had on a field jacket over my summer uniform, and I told him it was all I had. He said he was going to put me "on report" [under restriction pending military action]. I said, loud enough for the other people standing around to hear, that yesterday, I was in Vietnam, and I had just arrived home! Before he could reply, people started cursing the major, and he slunk away. This was another wrinkle in the "welcome back to America."

It kept turning out to be an eventful day, a weird day, as Creigh moved from one side of the world to the other in less than two days, from one culture to another, from a war zone to a no-war zone, and with jet lag.

"As I waited for Beth to pick me up," Creigh remembered,

> ...another brother rat, Pete Goldman, appeared! I was stunned since he was the first stateside brother rat I encountered after my return. Pete said, "Where have you been?" I said, "Vietnam." As if not registering that I had just returned from Vietnam, Pete said, "I have to fly in a few minutes, but I wish I could show you my new Porsche." It seemed so out-of-body, and we laughed about that moment years later.

Once back in the US, Creigh had to get a new driver's license because, just before he left for Vietnam, his was revoked for speeding. He took the written test and easily passed it but failed the driving part because he didn't have both hands on the steering wheel while making a turn. "I was very surprised the officer flunked me," he said, "but I decided it wasn't over." Not one to let his veteran card go to waste, he said,

I turned toward this young guy in his Trooper hat and asked, "How old are you?" He said, "Why?" I said, "I just got back from Vietnam last week, and we're losing guys in big numbers. We need more young, healthy, strong men like you over there right now. I can help you get in the pipeline right away because I have contacts at the Pentagon. I just need your information and Social Security number. What do you say?" He looked at me, took the clipboard, scratched out the failing grade, and passed me. He never said another word and left.

Creigh had served in the Army for 1.5 years and still had 2.5 more years of obligatory service. Assigned to West Germany, he and Beth arrived in the middle of January 1971. They were placed in temporary quarters since their off-post apartment wasn't ready. And that is when the next strange and scary thing happened.

Beth and Creigh were settling in for the evening that first night when there was a loud banging on the door. Sensing possible danger, Creigh grabbed a knife, ushered Beth into one of the bedrooms, and showed her how to block the door with a chair wedge. He returned to the front door and shouted that he was a first lieutenant and had already called the military police. Someone on the other side of the door replied, "You're not a first lieutenant, and you are not supposed to be in this apartment!" Creigh replied, "I have orders in my hand that state I am authorized to be here." The other side shouted, "We don't believe you!" Creigh, with nerves still in combat mode from Vietnam, threatened, "I'm going to open the door, and if you're not standing at attention, I'll cut the first person I see to defend my family!" With his heart racing, he opened the door and heard footsteps slapping on the descending stairs. One guy was standing at attention in a military police fatigue uniform. Creigh demanded his name and unit, which he provided.

The next day, Creigh went to that MP company's orderly room. A noncommissioned officer opened the door. Creigh demanded to see the commanding officer. He noticed the CO's door, closed, to his left. With protests rising from the noncommissioned officer, Creigh went through the CO's door and confronted the captain. He told him what happened the night before. "Amid my outburst, he tried to get me to stand at attention. I refused and then left," Creigh relayed.

Later that day, Creigh reported to his new unit to sign in. The executive officer, the second in command, had heard what happened. "He said the commanding general wanted me to report to him immediately. I figured that was the end of my short career."

> When I reported to him, he put me at ease and explained that I had been caught in the middle of an undercover drug investigation. He noted that I should have been more respectful to the MP officer, but I was not "on report." It turns out that the MP captain was part of the drug ring! The apartment had been a place for hash heads and dopers to hang out. Then he said he would like me to be his aide. I politely declined and said maybe it would be better to just send me back to Vietnam, where I knew how to do things.

The next 2.5 years in Germany, January 1971 to August 1973, were less eventful. His days were filled with the usual military peacetime service. In the summer of 1971, Creigh took the Graduate Record Exams (GRE). The US Army, in cooperation with the University of Maryland and the University of Southern California, had created two graduate programs in West Germany. Creigh had decided to earn a master's degree in international relations and had an interview with the head of the USC Department of International Relations, Dr. Lawrence Whetton. Dr. Whetton was curious about why Creigh had low grades at VMI and yet had scored in the top 5 percent on the GRE. Creigh explained, "Sir, I was not very interested in studying while at VMI. I knew I would come out as a second lieutenant and focused on keeping my grades up enough to run varsity cross-country and track." Dr. Whetton gave him a conditional acceptance, saying he had to immediately show A and B grades in his classes, which he did.

For the next twenty months, Creigh commuted two or three nights a week from Neu Ulm to attend his master's classes in Augsburg and Munich while also serving as an artillery captain, battery commander, and a staff officer in his battalion.

Completing his military obligation in the late summer of 1973, Creigh and Beth returned to Atlanta, Georgia, where he completed his thesis on international terrorism. He successfully stood for his orals and written examinations in Munich and received his master of arts in international relations in February 1974. They built a house in Atlanta, and their first child, Rebecca, was born in 1976.

In Atlanta, Creigh took a temporary job with a company called Lendman that organized hiring conventions while deciding what to do next. Creigh's job was to travel to military bases throughout the southeast to recruit attendees. He learned public speaking, how to use a microphone, and how to travel efficiently, all skills that contributed to his next chapter in life.

Creigh decided he needed to take up running again. One of his friends suggested that he needed new shoes. As life would have it, his need for new shoes tipped the scales in the direction of a new career, which was not an adviser on international terrorism! His friend directed him to a running store called Phidippides in Atlanta. Creigh thought it was crazy to have a store just for runners. On his first shopping visit there, he met great runners, including the 1972 US Olympian Jeff Galloway. Jeff took Creigh under his wing, and his next life adventure began. Jeff coached Creigh for free, and Creigh became a decent recreational runner, loving being back in the sport. Phidippides became his new hangout.

In the spring of 1978, Creigh told Jeff that he wanted to open his own running store in Atlanta. Jeff discouraged the idea, as Atlanta was already saturated with such stores, but suggested he consider opening a store in Denver, Colorado. Since Creigh also loved to ski,

Denver was perfect! Without telling Beth, Creigh said yes.

After a few trips to Denver, Creigh partnered with his friend, Phil Lawes, to build a store and jumped in headfirst. Starting their new business in August 1978, the learning curve was difficult. Creigh had learned to be a great promoter, but he described himself as a terrible retail person. They lost money and almost went bankrupt, but he kept creating different ways to survive. To develop a customer base for the shop, he created a road race event management company named BKB Limited and got people to sign up for races. For further income, he became an agent for world-class distance runners, getting them endorsements, prize money, and appearance money. He represented athletes from Great Britain, Canada, Kenya, America, Columbia, and New Zealand. He became an event announcer and radio/TV commentator, applying the leadership skills he learned at VMI, in the Army, and with Lendman.

Early in 1979, Creigh realized that he needed to be associated with organizations governing track and field and long-distance running at the highest national levels to get high-level announcing jobs. With some sage advice from new friends, he began to attend national meetings of The Athletics Congress, today known as USA Track and Field, which also selects USA Olympic teams. He became president of the Colorado Association and, in 1984, the National Chairman of Long Distance Running. With this new visibility, Creigh began getting announcing jobs throughout the US. During this time, his son, Meade, was born.

With his career in the running world taking off, Creigh sold his store in 1985, and his third child Page was born. His company, BKB Limited, was rocking. At the same time, his marriage was failing—Beth had filed for divorce. "I was reeling in private but looked solid in my public career," Creigh explained.

The divorce was expensive and bitter for a while, but Creigh said that he and Beth have since reconciled and enjoy each other's friendship. "More importantly," he said, "we made an early decision never to visit our personal differences in front of our three young children. It was the smartest decision we could have possibly made. We shared joint custody, and our children today are the most precious part of our friendship and relationship."

Keeping himself visible at the national level of running, Creigh stayed on the board of USA Track and Field for over twenty years. Multiple USA national teams that traveled to Japan, Denmark, Greece, and South Korea, selected him to be their manager or coach. For the next five years, Creigh kept representing athletes, increased his TV and public announcing, and continued to train and race at the recreational level.

In 1991, Creigh remarried and became president of a new chip timing †††† company called Winning Time USA (but Italian-owned), and he franchised it across the US from 1994-2004. At the same time, another international group, the Skyrunning Federation, out of Italy, asked him to join their board, and they were able to travel to events as close as Aspen, Colorado, and as far as France, Italy, and Mexico. These were fun days and gave him even more exposure to the world of running.

In 1997, the Leukemia Society, Rocky Mountain Region, asked Creigh to organize a marathon on the island of Cozumel to raise money for the organization. One board member had a beautiful home in Cozumel, and for the next three years, Creigh spent time in that home planning and conducting the Cozumel Marathon and the Cozumel Triathlon. They were also set for the fall of 2001 when Al Qaeda attacked the Twin Towers in New York. Not knowing what the political and security fallout might be, they canceled the event. After the fallout subsided, they returned to planning for 2005 when Hurricane Wilma hit. That was the end of the Cozumel adventure. Despite these setbacks, they raised over a million dollars for the

---

†††† Chip timing systems require that athletes wear a small, lightweight chip that uniquely identifies them as they cross strategically placed, electronic mats.

Leukemia Society (now the Leukemia and Lymphoma Society) through various subsequent events. In the middle of the Cozumel adventure, in 1999, Creigh became a founding member of Running USA, now the leading nonprofit running industry organization. He remained on their board for over twelve years and was honored to be in their National Hall of Champions.

Creigh loved starting companies, and in 2003, he and a friend, Rob Klingensmith, started a photography company, Verismile, in partnership with Kodak and won a photography contract for the twenty-fifth anniversary of the Iron Man Triathlon that year. "It was a flash success for two years until the much larger photography companies significantly underbid us and forced us out of the market."

He was still president of the Italian-owned company Winning Time, which used chips to time races. In 2002, they timed a race in Greece at the Athens Marathon. While this was huge for Winning Time and BKB Limited, the Italian owner did not manage the company well, and in 2002, Creigh quit the board.

At Christmas that same year, Creigh surprised his wife of twelve years, Annie, with a trip to Kenya to visit his friend, Peter Tanui, a Kenyan runner, and do some training runs with great Kenyan athletes. They left for Kenya in February 2003. This was when Creigh's life began to change toward humanitarian causes.

Peter encouraged Creigh and Annie to visit his primary school in his village of Kipture. Peter was the only primary school graduate from his village who had made his way to America and graduated from college. While Creigh was hesitant to go, Peter insisted. The headmaster, teachers, and 500 students were very welcoming. They walked the modest grounds, a field with one-story buildings. As they approached a low rock wall that encompassed some vegetation, Creigh asked the headmaster if that was a garden. "No," he replied, "that is where God will provide a library someday." Surprised, Creigh asked, "Where is your library now?" The headmaster opened a nearby door, and inside a narrow room, old British books were crammed from floor to ceiling. Creigh was stunned. They walked on and saw some women in the distance working around what appeared to be a fire. Creigh, woefully naïve about Kenyan public schools, asked, "Is that where you burn your garbage?" "No," replied the headmaster, "that is where we prepare ugali [stiff maize flour porridge] for the children's lunch." "Where is the dining hall?" asked Creigh. "We don't have a kitchen or a dining hall." Impulsively, Creigh turned to Peter and said, "We need to form a nonprofit organization to raise money to build a library and a kitchen." Within minutes of this comment, the headmaster led Creigh into a meeting of school leaders and announced, "Mr. Kelley is going to build a library and kitchen for us!" There it was—a commitment! Another new chapter in Creigh's life opened.

Upon returning to Colorado, Creigh began to honor his commitment to the Kipture Primary School. He cobbled an application for the Kipture Primary School Foundation and submitted it to the Colorado Secretary of State. Two years earlier, on September 11, 2001, Al Qaeda had attacked and demolished the Twin Towers in New York City. The US had formed the Department of Homeland Security in November 2002 to trace US funds that may have flowed to Al Qaeda, the Middle East organization responsible for the attack. All funds going to Africa or the Middle East were suspect. Thus, five months later, an agent from the Internal Revenue Service called Creigh and asked why he was creating a foundation. Creigh replied that it was all on the application. The IRS agent said, "I have to ask you, are you perhaps working with other groups in Africa that could use the money for other purposes?" "Look at the photos," Creigh replied. "They show clearly what the foundation is for." The agent continued, "They could have been photoshopped." Now Creigh was irritated. He asked the agent, "Do you have a passport?" "Why?" the agent asked. "If you do, ask your boss to let me fly you to Kenya with your camera, and you take the pictures. I'll use my private money to have you do this!" "I'll call you back," the agent replied. Three weeks later, the document for the new foundation arrived in the mail.

Creigh, Annie, Peter, and Peter's brother raised funds to build the school library and begin work on the kitchen. They returned to Kenya in early 2005 and saw the fruits of their labor. A library building stood where there was once a narrow closet, and a building was being completed that would serve as the dining hall and kitchen. They also visited a nearby medical clinic, a rudimentary building, offering primary care, which later became important to the foundation as well.

At this point, Creigh was greatly satisfied with his life. He had a successful career as an agent for athletes, an organizer of running events, and an event announcer. He had a nonprofit raising funds to improve a primary school in Kenya. And he thought he had a great marriage to a wonderful woman. He was at the top of his game. But, in the summer of 2005, Annie surprised Creigh by filing for divorce. Their fifteen-year marriage had suddenly and unexpectedly ended. Less than a year later, Annie married one of Creigh's contract staff. Creigh vowed never again to marry. Two of his three children had completed college—one was near graduation—and now he would concentrate on his career, which he loved. No, he would never fall in love again and certainly never remarry. That did not last long.

Creigh met Renee Hamilton through a mutual friend in February 2006. "Through a God wink, we fell in love," he said. After a sixteen-year friendship, they announced their engagement in the summer of 2022 and plan to be married in Kenya in 2024.

Creigh's life continued to have high points and low points. In 2009, he was inducted into the Colorado Running Hall of Fame. But then came the bad news, in 2012, that he had cancer. He was shocked; he was in the best running condition in over ten years. After the removal of a kidney and rounds of chemotherapy, doctors told him his cancer was stage four. For a while, he felt the end was near. However, his doctor insisted that he could endure heavy doses of chemo since he was in such great shape. And indeed, he got better. By mid-February 2013, he had no evidence of cancer. The only lasting side-effect was that he was unable to enjoy fast running. That was better than the alternative!

Creigh continued his various business endeavors until 2016 when he sold his business and saw retirement just around the corner. But "life has a way of getting in the way of well-made plans," he reflected. By 2018, he was back, trying to save the company he had sold, as it had failed before the new owner had completed all the payouts. He still had to announce gigs and local running events to tide him over until he could "close the skeleton of . . . [his] once thriving BKB Limited and march on."

Creigh continues to be race director of the Denver Colfax Marathon weekend, which reached almost 20,000 entrants in 2019. The COVID-19 pandemic resulted in the cancellation of marathons in 2020 and 2021. During the pandemic shutdown, Creigh and the CEO of the Denver Colfax Marathon wrote "best practices" for recreational running and walking events. It became an open-source document used by hundreds of events across the US and in some foreign countries. The National Sports Safety and Security Organization awarded the two authors a national award for their work in 2021. Further, in November 2021, the National Race Directors' Meeting in Florida honored Creigh with a National Lifetime Achievement Award.

Creigh continues to announce some major events across the US. "I'm very happy and excited to have a microphone in my hands," he said.

LOOKING BACK

While Creigh found VMI tough, to the point of sometimes crying, he looks back on the experience as one of building character and leadership:

> Frankly, I credit VMI for giving me the basis for leadership skills that have served me reasonably well throughout my career. We learned how to work through adverse conditions. I credit VMI for giving me the strength and ingenuity to

overcome seemingly impossible obstacles. "Never say die!" always resonates with me. My love of the Institute has grown with each successive year. It takes perspective through the lens of time to fully understand how the harsh environment and the unwavering commitment to honor and duty provided a significant payout over the following decades. It is hard to imagine how I would have fared at a more normal college. My guess is that I would have been less of a leader and a person. My sense of honor and my loyalty to my brother rats are two of the finest elements I have been blessed with.

In 1996, the United States sued the state of Virginia and VMI, alleging that VMI's exclusively male admission policy violated the Fourteenth Amendment's Equal Protection Clause. I asked Creigh what he felt about the controversy during that period. He replied,

> It never bothered me to have female cadets since I always admired the Israeli military model. I knew women could fit right in. I remember saying at the time, "If women are crazy enough to want to be a VMI cadet, we should be smart enough to accept them and take their money!" I felt that if Black cadets could weather the Institute's storm of disparaging remarks and racist comments in the Rat Line, women could equally survive the misogynistic and disparaging language thrown at them. The "tough get tougher, and the weak fall away." Outsiders may not like that dark model, but it is a great preparation (if you survive it) for the world they would walk into upon graduation. Most of us knew the admission of women was an inevitable change, just as it had been for the US service academies.

Creigh surmises that VMI fought the inclusion of women to maintain the allegiance of the older alumni who gave considerable wealth to the Institute. "The Institute could always argue that it had to comply with the 'law of the land,' so the alumni who didn't like the decision would recognize that the Institute had 'fought the good fight,' and they would continue to give their wealth to VMI," Creigh reflected. He feels that the admission of Black and female cadets was "natural and unequivocally positive." Creigh added,

> We had other ethnic groups admitted to VMI almost a century before the first Black cadet without incident. Being a minority at VMI wasn't new to the Institute. The cadets singled out anyone who stood out, positively or negatively. In a minor way, I was singled out as a "Yankee." I had to reconcile that almost every day in the Rat Line and find other ways to survive. Every new cadet had to do the same.

I asked Creigh about his thoughts on the Civil War symbols, statues, and rituals on post. He replied,

> When I was a cadet, I never equated slavery with VMI. It simply wasn't taught, and I never thought of Jackson or any other iconic Civil War heroes as racist or slaveholders. The painting of the cadets at the Battle of New Market made a huge impression on me, and I thought of those cadets as extraordinary. I still believe they were. I remember thinking that, regardless of my personal view about fighting in Vietnam, I resolved that I would follow legal orders and not question my country's position. I believe that was true of VMI faculty and cadets during the Civil War. I never thought of Lee, or anyone who fought for the Confederacy, as traitors. I knew slavery was a failed concept and practice, but I believed that the central purpose of the fight was "states' rights," as my mother and other Southern relatives taught me. It took me a long time to reconcile the difference.

Creigh said he opposed the removal of the Jackson statue because Jackson had been a great leader in the Civil War and had given up his slaves much earlier. "His work to educate young Black children was notable since it was not condoned in the South. However, he was an unremarkable professor."

Regarding the VMI Honor Code, Creigh feels that "it was the best element for life instruction. The importance of ethics and honest behavior cannot be underestimated in a world that condones unethical practices and dishonesty for convenient shortcuts."

"Honor is a tough but uncompromising standard. It is a 'perfect world' aspiration, and once you understand it, it's easy to comply," Creigh said. "You try to model honor in your day-to-day personal and professional life. I often thought about it when making difficult decisions."

As for the "single sanction" VMI Honor Code, Creigh has always been for it. He explained,

> There is only one kind of honor. I saw different standards in the business and military worlds. If you lied, cheated, or stole, and were caught, the consequences were different. You might lose rank or a job, be reassigned, pay a fine, or be put in jail. The consequences were not as catastrophic as a cadet being dismissed due to a VMI Honor Code violation. I believe the absolute doctrine at VMI has helped many graduates make better decisions in their personal and professional lives because they have a sharper sense of the consequences of bad behavior.

Another part of the harsh life at VMI is the Rat Line. Creigh described it as "cruel, debasing, and leveling. It has a clear purpose, in my opinion: throw everything you can at these young neophytes and see who can survive. Those who do will be better for it." Creigh believes the Rat Line

> ... removed any status you might have enjoyed in your time prior to VMI, and the only way to go was up. We were all the same at the bottom of the heap. It helped me earn the "distinguished military student" title after summer camp. Although I was always a private in rank at VMI, I think the resilient training of hard day-to-day life at VMI, and certainly in the Rat Line, validated that VMI could produce leaders from any group of cadets, regardless of position.

Creigh also said that VMI prepared him for Vietnam. He said his service in Vietnam wasn't as hard as the Rat Line! He believes that harassment of rats is, and was, the right thing to do:

> It's not intended to be fair or pleasant. It intends to strip away your former comforts and see what you are truly made of. I learned that I could escape the Rat Line once I exited the barracks and headed to class, the mess hall, or preferably to cross-country or track practice. Those were my "freedom" zones, and I knew I could survive the rest of the actions in barracks.

Creigh said he knew almost nothing about the history of VMI before he went there other than his mother's comments about how she loved going to VMI hops. He never paid much attention to the actual history until the flareups caused by *Washington Post* journalist Ian Shapira's caustic appraisal of VMI, beginning in mid-2020. "I was conflicted," he replied, "and I discounted much of what was being said by disgruntled cadets. Every class had embittered graduates. It's not a perfect society. I follow the ongoing debates about changes already put in place and am hopeful whatever future changes implemented will be reasonable and fair."

As for VMI's future, Creigh says his conversations with the new Superintendent General Wins and cadets have been very positive and reassuring. "I believe the cadets are doing their best not to get embroiled in the dissonance propagated by journalists who take a dim view of VMI. Cadets seem to appreciate the benefits of VMI, and the present group of cadets is exemplary."

THE BEST AND WORST OF LIFE

★ ★ ★

"Everything that happens to a person provides instruction for the future. Difficulty makes a person stronger if the person stays positive."
—A graduate, Class of '68

Life has its rewards and challenges, and almost no one has a perfect life or escapes tragedy. There is a saying that *if nothing bad has ever happened to you, just wait, it will.*

In 2018, the members of the Class of '68 were about seventy-two years old. They were at the time of life when adults often look back on their lives and ask themselves whether it was a life well lived. What did they learn from their journey? I asked them to probe their lives, their feelings, their values, their mistakes, and their life lessons.

The men chose to focus on their values, in particular honesty, integrity, trustworthiness, and maintaining one's honor. They applied these values to their military service, careers, and marriages. They attributed their personal failures, for the most part, to straying from this path of values. Their answers were so honest that they often included examples of their personal failures, blaming themselves for the loss of a marriage or losing a job. While many of the men were clearly highly accomplished, not one bragged about himself. To explain why they so valued honor, several men said that in the military, and especially in combat, lives depend upon holding up a code of honor. And this is why VMI has a "single sanction" policy for breaking the Honor Code. "Drumming out" is a harsh punishment for any cadet, but honesty can be a matter of life and death.

Another value that the men frequently mentioned was respect for others. They were living with White young men like themselves while at VMI. Those were the times. All schools in Virginia in the early and mid-1960s were racially segregated. Asians and Jewish cadets were admitted, but their numbers were very low. The cadets did not experience a diversity of other races and certainly not women, but when they went out into the real world, they soon learned that success as a leader required respect for all people, no matter their race, color, or gender. Many said they wished that VMI had been more diverse when they were cadets, and they feel that the admission of women and cadets of color is one of the best changes VMI has made since their graduation.

Here is a summary of the good and bad things that happened in the lives of the Class of '68.

THE BEST

All but 10 men out of 121 said that marrying their wives and having children were the most wonderful events in their lives: happy family life, loving marriages, successful children, and watching grandchildren grow.

"Finding and keeping a loving companion. Seeing our daughter overcome problems in her late teens to become a successful wife, mother, and businessperson," said one.

"Seeing my children grow and mature and avoiding major pitfalls (drugs, addictions, crime, divorce) and for me to have a wonderful international career and see my wife also have a wonderful international career and experiencing life together around the world. Now experiencing the growth and maturing of my grandchildren," wrote another.

Several men named a successful career, attending VMI, maintaining friendships with classmates, traveling, and seeing many cultures as their best experiences.

A few mentioned retirement as the best thing that has happened to them; a couple mentioned volunteer work, and two said surviving Vietnam.

One man wrote, "Surviving 200-plus missions in Vietnam. Marrying my wife. Watching my kids grow up and succeed in life. Traveling the world for international business."

Another said, "The joy (plus occasional pain) and excitement of fatherhood, with four loving children and three grandsons. The joy of success as an athlete throughout my life and pulling both my mother and father into that arena throughout high school and college. Accolades in business throughout my career. The magnificent friendships I've created. And the understanding and belief that God has forgiven me my trespasses."

Others wrote the following: "Getting married, becoming a Christian, becoming a father, enjoyable work, retirement."

"Becoming a VMI alumnus. Marrying and enjoying life with my other half since 1974. Enjoying an outstanding career. Enjoying our children becoming responsible adults and parents."

However, life being what it is, no one escapes some kind of suffering, some kind of misfortune. So it was with this group of men.

THE WORST

American culture has its share of common addictions, and some in this group reported addictions. Eight men said they suffered from food addiction, five from sex addiction, five from pornography addiction, and one from gambling addiction. Seven of the men said they had not yet successfully overcome their mental health problem and are still working on recovery. All the others claimed success through counseling, talking with their wives, attending support groups, and realizing the harm they were doing to themselves and others. Some attended twelve-step programs for addictions, and others mentioned they were helped by reaching out to God. One had gastric bypass surgery.

By far, the most common negative event in their lives was the death of a loved one. Forty-seven men reported that they had lost a close family member, and nine men had lost a child. Two had children who committed suicide. Four men had been widowed. The remainder of the group had lost parents, siblings, and grandchildren. One reported that his father had murdered his mother and how traumatic this was for him. Twenty men reported the loss of close friends, five of whom were lost in combat.

Those who lost loved ones said death is something we must accept as part of the circle of life. It hurts and continues to hurt for a long time, but deaths also help us appreciate the time we have on earth, and we should live every day to its fullest. One wrote, "Life goes on, so one must look to the future, not the past. Time heals the sadness."

The next most common terrible thing that happened in their lives was divorce. Though some people claim that divorce can be a good thing—because it ends an unpleasant, and maybe even harmful, relationship—all eighteen men who reported divorce said things like this:

"My divorce separated me from my children and caused financial pain for everyone."

"Divorce was very painful to everyone involved."

"The most awful thing that happened in my life was the announcement by my first wife that she wanted a divorce (didn't see that coming)!"

"For me, the worst thing was the heartache and pain I caused my children and their spouses when I divorced their mother."

"Divorce followed by estrangements of family and close friends."

One man reported that "nearly losing [his] marriage because of [his] own immature and selfish actions."

Several men commented on the pain of divorce. They learned

that "it is important to recognize the truly important relationships that one has and not to jeopardize them through immature and selfish acts." Others wrote the following:

"My selfish acts almost destroyed my family, and I learned not to commit them anymore."

"I destroyed thirty-four years of marriage to the right person. Seek physical and mental health before you reach the point of no return."

"Divorce in my midthirties changed the course of my life. It affected my family as well as my finances. I realized that perseverance and discipline would get me through the crisis."

"Divorce is a reminder that being able to live with another human being requires some sacrifice."

Of those who had served in the military, several had served in Vietnam. Sixteen men suffered from post-traumatic stress disorder (PTSD). They wrote:

"The worst thing that happened to me was receiving orders for Vietnam on September 21, 1969, and our first child born September 20, 1969."

"I had to leave one of my men down in an ambush kill zone."

"Multiple wounds in Vietnam, forcing me out of the Army and leaving me permanently unable to physically accomplish many things I would have enjoyed."

"The several times when I knew I was going to die in Vietnam."

"The worst day of my life occurred in Vietnam when I was nearly killed by incoming mortar fire on a Fire Support Base. Nothing else in my life would I consider being close to that."

"Nearly getting killed a few times."

One reported the long separations from his wife and family during military service as his worst experience.

Some with PTSD were on medications under the care of the Veterans Administration. "The VA has me on medication for PTSD so that I can get to sleep instead of visiting Vietnam every night," said one.

Ten men reported losing their jobs as terrible events, and another ten reported serious physical illnesses.

Three men said that leaving VMI before graduating was a terrible thing for them. One admitted being "boned out" from too many demerits.

Another three said their worst things were failure to attain their own expected goals or ideals.

One wrote, "At various points in time, I discovered how close I came to the standards of ideals I held. It's painful to discover you don't measure up to your own standards."

And another wrote, "My experiences at VMI stunted my ability to show empathy to my family. My failure as a parent to understand how to parent children who did not see the world as I did. I regret the rough road my children and first wife had with me setting the standards for performance and behavior. I know I was not prepared for marriage and children. I failed as a parent as a result."

Two reported legal problems as being the worst. Another two said not getting promotions that they expected. Two said being deceived was the worst: "Being taken in by an evil person," and "Lies, deceit, scheming, hatred, bigotry, disrespect, abuse, betrayal, backstabbing," but without further explanation. Three reported problems in their marriages. One said his wife had addictions to drinking and gambling, and two men's wives were unfaithful.

One man said his daughter's estrangement from him was his worst event. Another said it was the incarceration of his son. One man was arrested once for driving under the influence of alcohol, and a final one said he discovered that he was woefully unprepared for college right out of high school.

The Class of '68 said they learned a great many life lessons from their worst experiences. Several men wrote something like this:

"Life is not a permanent arrangement. It is always changing and is both predictable and unpredictable. You must adapt because there is no choice."

Many men mentioned the theme of accepting that we cannot control everything that happens in life. We must recover from bad experiences, learn from them, and then move on.

Some wrote the following: "Everything that happens to a person provides instruction for the future. Difficulty makes a person stronger if the person stays positive."

"My failures hurt and were embarrassing, but I learned from the experiences."

"I learned a lot from the not-so-good times."

"Live as well as you possibly can, be happy, avoid toxic people/places, and seek joy and the 'lightness of being.'"

Those who were fired from their jobs said being let go made them better employees and employers.

Those who suffered terrible injuries or illnesses said the experience gave them an appreciation for life and good health. They had to put their misfortune into perspective, realizing that some other people were suffering more and that many of their colleagues had died, so they felt lucky even to be alive. Several said we should do all we can to stay healthy.

Those who had been betrayed by a spouse or colleague said that we should never trust other people. One wrote that it took him years to trust a woman again. Several others said it is best to trust ourselves over others, to trust our own instincts, and to realize that not everyone has the same standard of ethics that they learned at VMI.

Based on their own life experiences, these men offered plenty of advice to future cadets and to the Institute.

CLASS OF '68 ADVICE TO FUTURE CADETS

★ ★ ★

"Get a coffee mug and have inscribed on one side 'Honor Above Self' and on the other side 'You may be whatever you resolve to be.' Live by those principles, and you will have a full and valuable life."
—A graduate, Class of '68

Looking over their lives of seventy-two years, the Class of 1968 offered the following advice to current and future VMI cadets: Take more courses, get an advanced degree, read widely, see the world, and get out of your comfort zone because, in doing so, you can change course when companies close or a job ceases.

ACCEPT NEW CHALLENGES

The Class of '68 recommended cadets be constantly learning, accepting new challenges, adapting, and changing themselves.

"Have a buffet of skills that can be turned into business endeavors."

"Keep your knowledge as current as possible."

The men recommended not being afraid of failure because everyone has failures at one time or another, and these are learning opportunities. They said things like this:

"Everybody fails—learn and grow from your failures."

"Expect the unexpected."

"Be prepared to deal with many changes throughout your personal and working life."

"Be prepared to embrace change and challenges."

MARRY WELL

Repeatedly mentioned was the importance of marrying well:

"Marry wisely and well."

"Locate and marry your best friend who will be with you forever in this life."

"Wait till you're over thirty to marry. Be sure to claim YOUR life before you marry. You will make a far better husband and father."

"Find someone to love who will complete you."

"If you're lucky enough to get married, dedicate yourself to making that marriage work. If you're blessed with children, be prepared to spend unbelievably large amounts of time being a parent. Discipline firmly without abusing, which will mean learning to control your temper."

SAVE AND INVEST

They recommended saving and investing money and using money for good purposes. "But don't pursue money for the sake of selfish desires. Give back when you can."

KEEP YOUR FRIENDS

They suggested maintaining ties with brother rats, family, and friends:

"Appreciate your family. Be loyal to your friends. Appreciate your brother rats."

"Remember your BRs and love and support each other. They are more important than you know, and as a group, you are stronger than the one."

"Keep in contact with old friends: those you make at VMI, those you had before you came to VMI, and those you meet later in life."

NEVER GIVE UP

They said the great lesson to be taken from VMI is never to give up, even when things are looking bad:

"Life will go in directions you don't expect. VMI gives you the experience and confidence to persevere in difficult situations."

"Life is an uphill battle, just like their careers at VMI. Never give up!"

"Stay the course, graduate, and stay true to your principles."

"Never quit, not once. Hard the first time but gets easier each time. Never, ever quit."

"You can be whatever you resolve to be if you work hard and don't ever give up. VMI taught me to not have a reverse gear. Don't look back except to learn from previous errors so that you don't repeat mistakes. Life is for the present and the future. If you have a goal, don't ever give up."

"When things are bad, expect them to get better! Don't quit, don't give up, persevere! Try to do what is right, even if it isn't fashionable! The guy at the bottom of the pyramid is often more responsible for the team's success than the guy at the top!"

STAY POSITIVE

Men emphasized the importance of staying positive. Many said things like this:

"Learn to be optimistic about the future. Always give younger folks who work with you a chance to be successful."

"Stay positive and optimistic and do not whine."

ADHERE TO VMI TRAINING

Most of the men advised adhering to VMI's training: retaining a strong work ethic, remaining honest and tolerant, and embracing diversity and challenges:

"As a VMI graduate, you enter a complex and challenging world armed with the tools to overcome adversity and be successful in whatever vocation you pursue. Our Honor Code is an anchor, and you should continue to abide by it with the understanding that many of the people you will encounter do not live by the principles of the code."

"Never give up, and trust in your training. Always continue to learn and be loyal to yourself, friends, occupation, God, and the bond to your brother rats! Honor above self."

"Your experience at VMI is one of your greatest life assets. Because of your education and time at VMI, you will be presented with many opportunities in your life. Be careful which opportunities you choose to experience, as those choices will affect your life path and the availability of additional opportunities."

"Savor the memories of your four years at VMI. It will instill the values of duty, integrity, and loyalty."

FOLLOW THE VMI HONOR SYSTEM THROUGH LIFE

The VMI Honor System undoubtedly made a huge impact on their lives. They wrote:

"Always follow the VMI Honor Code in all aspects of life. I actually quit a company due to its lack of ethics in upper management."

"The VMI Honor System is heart and soul of our school."

"Never forget who you are or where you came from. Live the Honor Code, and while you may suffer occasionally for your integrity, it is the one thing no one can take from you. It is, however, easy and tragic to lose honor. Same goes for loyalty."

"Never forget what they taught you at VMI."

And one man wrote more extensively:

> Live the VMI Honor Code. You may not be popular with all people, but you will be respected by those who matter. You will positively influence people and events in ways you may never know, but your influence will matter. Deal in truth. This is a little different from being honorable per our Honor Code. This entails seeking truth and dealing with it (honorably) to include, for example: our founding principles of life, liberty, and the pursuit of happiness . . . and slavery. Understanding

how slavery and its inherent injustice came to exist in America is one thing; failure to do our part today to help alleviate injustice is different. Let us each strive to achieve a "more perfect union" day by day in every relationship. Brave VMI cadets and alumni fought for the Confederacy, and some died "on the field of honor." Their courage merits respect. Their cause, as we currently understand it, does not.

They advised all cadets to put honor above self:

"As at VMI, do your duty and place honor above self. Love your family and country, and do not lie, cheat, or steal."

"Always be honorable and true to the promises you give."

"Live honorably. Be true to the values instilled by your parents, faith, and VMI."

TREAT OTHERS WITH RESPECT

Many said to always treat others with respect:

"Never lose a sense of compassion."

"Treat people with dignity and respect."

"Recognize that others may see things differently. Be tolerant."

"Treat others as you would have them treat you."

"Be honest with all that you encounter. Be friendly and greet all with a smile. Be open-minded and tolerant."

BE A LEADER

They emphasized leadership in their advice to cadets:

"Aspire to be a leader. Not just in the military but in other fields as well. Leadership means having credibility. Don't ask your people to do something you can't, haven't, or won't do yourself. Especially important in the military."

HAVE A SPIRITUAL LIFE

Several of the men advised having a spiritual life. They wrote things like this:

"Success in life is not just about material things. Your relationship with God is much more important."

PRACTICE INTEGRITY

The men recommended cadets practice integrity throughout life:

"Maintain your personal integrity. If you lose it, it is very hard to regain it. In your heart of hearts, you know what is right, so do it and do not be dissuaded!"

"Never sacrifice your ethics and honesty for any price."

"Have the courage to speak up and take action for what you believe is right."

"Take responsibility for what you do in all aspects of your life, and do the right thing in every aspect as well."

THE WORLD IS NOT LIKE VMI

On the other hand, many advised future cadets to recognize that VMI is not necessarily reflective of the real world, so it is important to learn how to adapt to different situations while retaining the core values of VMI:

"Don't expect the people you encounter to always share your beliefs or commitment. You will need to learn how to adapt to this without compromising your own standards."

"VMI is a mixed experience; keep what was valuable for your own growth and discard what was not. It may take some years to understand what was valuable and what was not."

And finally, a longer admonition:

> The real world is not like VMI. Nobody cares about what you accomplished at VMI. You enter the world with a clean slate—unless you suck up to alumni for your job, in which case you might have a biased sponsor for a while. Some people dislike military school graduates, believe it or not. And VMI is not a service academy—some people care about that. Don't believe all the hype about how unique and

wonderful you are. All colleges think that, especially if they have great winning sports programs. It is not fun watching VMI get its ass kicked all the time, even if you are a loyal alum. VMI is the only school with a fight song about getting beat included. On the other hand, you will have the unbelievable satisfaction of having endured four years of physical and academic challenges that few others can claim, although they will claim it. VMI is respected where it is known, but don't count on it for your success. Most important advice—it can never be as bad on the outside as it was on the inside. Take solace in that, when times get tough, it can only get better.

LIVE LIFE TO THE FULLEST

They advised living life to its fullest and not sweating the small stuff by prioritizing what is important:

"Live life to its fullest; one never knows how long he/she is given to experience it. Take nothing in life for granted. Each day is precious and should be enjoyed to the fullest."

"Go easy, have fun, and know that this life is all about peace, joy, love, and happiness."

"Be happy enjoying the road and not just the endpoint."

"Enjoy every day, as each day is precious."

"Go with the flow. Life is too short to let little things worry you too much."

"Prioritize duty, honor, country, and caring about family and friends. Work hard and smart and prioritize and balance your life, never forgetting the things that are most important."

"Be careful about what you take seriously."

"Use the VMI experience to examine yourself and your life. Find your center and nurture your inner life."

"Be true to yourself. Admit when you're wrong and be humble when right."

SET GOALS AND FOLLOW YOUR PASSION

The men also emphasized setting goals, having a firm sense of direction, and committing to whatever we choose to do. They said this:

"Learn to fill obligations to nation and others." And "Focus more on duty, less on wants."

"Find a job or profession you really love... something you would look forward to doing every day, even if you were not being paid. Stick to it!"

"Pursue the career field that you believe most matches your individual talents."

"Take a risk to find what you are most excited about. Find that 'something' that gets you fired up every day and pursue it, regardless of economic prospects. Find a 'job' or 'career path' that is challenging and rewarding (emotionally and physically). Don't end up in the latter years wishing you'd followed your dream but did not."

"Do something you love; make your vocation your vacation."

"Pursue your true interests and dreams."

"Follow your heart and don't be afraid to march to the beat of a different drummer."

"Don't be too quick on choosing your life's work. Go with the flow and make the choice when you are sure of what you want to do."

"Find work that you enjoy and that fulfills you."

"You'll have the opportunity to have at least three full and distinct twenty-year careers in your lifetime. Don't limit yourself."

"Life is full of challenges, but never give up on pursuing your goals/dreams."

A '68 graduate who followed his passions and dreams was Paul Hebert. He got out of his comfort zone, lived, worked around the world, and faced enormous challenges in his work while juggling a two-career marriage and two children.

PAUL HEBERT

* ★ *

CLASS OF '68, JONATHAN DANIELS HUMANITARIAN AWARD

VMI alumni today often say that VMI's two greatest graduates are George C. Marshall, Class of 1901, and Jonathan Daniels, Class of 1961. As mentioned earlier, VMI honors the legacy of both men with awards: the Marshall award, given every two years to a 1st Class cadet or rising 1st Class cadet, and the Daniels award, given around every five years to someone who has carried forward the Daniels legacy of civil rights and humanitarian work. The fourth recipient of this award was one of VMI's own—Paul Hebert.

Paul realized early in his career that he wanted to make a difference in the world by improving the living conditions of people in developing countries. After working in water supply and sanitation for two decades, he pivoted to direct humanitarian assistance in war zones, refugee camps, and famines. His early years growing up in segregated Virginia were influential in forming his attitudes toward helping others.

Paul was born and raised in Richmond, Virginia, in a very average middle-class home. His father, Julius, had moved to Richmond in his early twenties from Morgan City, Louisiana, to take a job at VEPCO (Virginia Electric and Power Company), where he met Paul's mother, Helen, who was also working there. Helen had completed two years at James Madison College in Harrisonburg, Virginia. Paul's childhood revolved around sports, mostly football.

By the time Paul reached high school, he was ready to play varsity football and became a star player at George Wythe High School. His senior year, VMI reached out to him with a football scholarship. It was not just football that drew Paul to VMI. He wanted to study engineering, and VMI was well-known in Virginia for its excellent engineering program.

Like other White children in the 1960s in Richmond, Paul went to an all-White high school and attended an all-White Episcopal Church. The only Black person he knew was a maid who came to their house to iron clothes once a week and people who worked in his father's truck stop. Unlike some other Richmond families, Paul's family was not steeped in Civil War or Confederate lore. "I never remember discussing anything about the Civil War in my family while growing up, perhaps because my father was from Louisiana," he said. Yet he remembers being very aware of the racial strife going on in Richmond, where there were regular demonstrations against segregation. In 1963, the Richmond public schools carried out what looked to be a pilot program in ending segregation. George Wythe High School admitted six Black students, handpicked behind the scenes, and one Black young man joined the football team. "I felt for them," Paul said, "being thrust into this all-White school of 2,000 students. As far as I know, all went well in our school for those Black kids." The Richmond schools were not fully integrated until 1970.

Julius's truck stop, with its restaurant, was a microcosm of the Jim

Crow system of the South. While working during summer breaks, from the age of fourteen, Paul was disturbed by the "Whites only" and "Coloreds only" signs applied to sections of the restaurant, the restrooms, and the entrances. When he asked his father if he had to have these signs, his father said, "I have no choice. It's the law here in Virginia." Several of his father's employees were Black, and Paul noted that Julius always treated them respectfully.

AT VMI

Before enrolling, Paul knew almost nothing about VMI, had never visited the place, knew no one who had gone to college there, and had no family background in the military. He knew that VMI was a highly respected state-supported college with a famous graduate, General George C. Marshall.

Paul's first few weeks at VMI were ones of surprise, dismay, and adjustment to such a different way of life. One of the first things he realized was that he was not all that special. While he had been top of the heap at George Wythe High School, student body president, star athlete, and high academic standing, there were plenty of those same stars at VMI. In addition, many of the young men had come from prominent families with historical ties to VMI and fathers who were high in the military. It was daunting and humbling—the great leveler. And then there was the Rat Line, the shouting, the push-ups, the straining, the "square meals," the endless marching. He explained that being on the football and track teams saved him from some of this:

> Athletics exempted me from much of what most of my classmates were required to do on the military side (drills, marching, extra running, and exercises) since we had football and track practice after classes every day, and we traveled away for many of our games. We slept in on Sundays following our home football games, which was a great privilege. We had a separate athletic table where we did

not have to eat a "square meal." We had to walk the Rat Line, straining when called upon, do push-ups at the command of upper-classmen, and stay on the fourth stoop except to visit the room of our 1st Class dykes. There, we could relax.

Paul soon discovered that he was not enamored with military life. However, he decided he would get a good education, play NCAA football, and graduate with an Army commission.

Even though the US was going through a strife-filled period between 1964 and 1968, with the war in Vietnam, daily protests against the war, and the civil rights struggle, Paul said he was living in the VMI bubble, not following the news very closely. The only TV on post was in the PX, but there was little time to hang out there. Radios were allowed, but there was little time to listen. The *Washington Post* was available if one had time to read it. He got caught up on the news when he went home for holiday breaks.

Paul does not recall hearing about the tragic and dramatic 1965 murder of Jonathan Daniels. "To my memory, it was never mentioned," he said. He also does not recall much discussion of current events in general, other than the Vietnam War, in ROTC classes. He remembers the passing of the 1965 Voting Rights Act and the end of Jim Crow laws in restaurants, restrooms, and public transportation, and he was pleased it had happened. He sympathized with the Black people who were trying to change the system. He said the racial strife in Virginia was a bit too much for him, and the atmosphere at VMI seemed to reflect the values of 100 years before. "It was during my years at VMI that I decided I would move away from Virginia after finishing my education. I couldn't see staying in such a racially charged state."

Because of the Vietnam War and its horrors, Paul began to sour on the military. He was not sure we should be fighting over there. "Enlisted soldiers who served as part of the ROTC training contingent referred to the Vietcong as 'gooks,' which dehumanized them. I hated that," he said. "At the time, I could not explain my feelings; I was just negative about the military intervention and the large loss of life in the conflict so far away from our own country."

As an engineering major, Paul is still dismayed that he did not know that Claudius Crozet had created the original curriculum for the engineering program at VMI. Although the dining hall at VMI was named for Crozet, the engineering faculty, to the best of his memory, did not explain Crozet's contribution to the Institute. At that time, the only formal recognition of Crozet as a founder was his gravestone that stood in front of the Preston Library, where he had been reinterred in 1942. But the gravestone gave no indication that Crozet was both a founder of the Institute and creator of the engineering program.

In the summer of 1967, Paul went to a six-week Army ROTC basic camp in Pennsylvania, where he was one of seven trainees out of several thousand young men selected to be company commanders. Another one of the seven was Rick Siegel, Paul's roommate. This selection was based on demonstrated leadership skills, physical fitness achievement, and military acumen, no doubt learned at VMI. "I don't recall that Rick and I were recognized for this achievement when we returned to VMI."

After basic camp, Paul began thinking seriously about his future. I, his girlfriend, had just returned from my summer experience, an educational group tour of Europe led by professors from the University of Richmond. I could hardly contain my enthusiasm from my six weeks of immersion in the arts, architecture, and history of Western civilization, and I told Paul how the trip had changed my view of the future. I decided to pursue a master's degree in anthropology. Paul thought his six weeks of military immersion paled in comparison. He listened intently and with much jealousy to all I had seen and learned. Paul had been reading about development needs in the "third world," especially the basics, such as potable water and adequate sanitation. He began to think that his engineering education and further study of water and sanitation might be the key to a career in international work. At the start of his last year at VMI, he consulted with engineering professor Jim Lamb, who had received his PhD in environmental engineering at the University of North Carolina's School of Public Health, Chapel Hill. He and Civil Engineering Department Head Colonel John Knapp, a VMI 1954 graduate, supported Paul's application to UNC. Dr. Lamb noted that several of the professors in that department had worked in water and sanitation in Africa and Asia and would provide ideas for seeking work in the developing world.

Paul graduated second in his civil engineering major. Upon graduation, he was commissioned as a second lieutenant, but he took a deferment from the military to attend graduate school. He looked forward to experiencing "real college life." "I remember feeling great relief on graduation day and being ready to move on to a new phase of life, one with a great deal of personal freedom," he said.

AFTER VMI

In the spring of 1969, Paul and I were married. Together, we continued our graduate degrees at UNC. In the summer of 1970, I won a scholarship to attend a field school in ethnographic methods in Ireland. Paul had completed his master's degree, and so the two of us took off for Dublin in late May. While I attended my course and conducted research on family life among Dublin's poor, Paul found employment with a biological anthropologist, collecting blood samples for a genetic study of Irish Travelers. Paul photographed their colorful lives—the covered wagons they lived in and their occupations. This is where his lifelong interest in photography developed. I also had Traveler families in my research and wrote a master's thesis on them. After a wonderful two months in Ireland, Paul and I traveled to France, Switzerland, Denmark, and the Netherlands. This was Paul's first international experience, and he caught the bug.

Back in Chapel Hill, Paul received orders to attend officers' basic training at Fort Sam Houston, Texas, to begin in January 1971 for four months and then serve in the Army Medical Corps at the Edgewood Arsenal in Maryland. Paul was upgraded to the rank of captain and served two years. His job took him all over the United States to inspect military bases and Army contract industries for environmental hazards. These two years were rewarding professionally, as he was responsible for managing other engineers, technicians, and staff.

In January 1973, upon release from military duty, Paul took an engineering job with the Bechtel Corporation in San Francisco, thinking that Bechtel would offer him the opportunity to work abroad. Once Paul was on board at Bechtel, it looked like his dream of working abroad would not materialize for several years, given Bechtel's policy. Although he was satisfied with the work and responsibilities, he soon realized that this was not where he wanted to be. At UNC, he studied under some well-known professors with links to the World Bank and the World Health Organization and was exposed to the needs of developing countries for water and sanitation. He wanted to go abroad. I wanted to earn a PhD in anthropology, which would require research in a foreign culture. Somehow, we needed to make this work for both of us.

After a year with Bechtel, the Near East Foundation (NEF), a US nonprofit located in New York, contacted Paul about a potential job in Iran. Paul had contacted NEF while still in the Army, but they were just now getting back to him. He would serve as an adviser to the Tehran School of Public Health and the Iranian Ministry of Health at their Medical Research Station in Dezful, Iran. So, I worked out that I could do my doctorate research in Iran. Paul was eager to take on his first foreign assignment.

Paul arrived in Dezful in March 1974 when the Shah of Iran was still in power. It was at the beginning of the hot season, where daily temperatures reach up to 120 degrees Fahrenheit, and slow-moving yellow dust storms are a frequent occurrence. Dezful is in the far south of Iran, in Khuzestan Province. It is a highly traditional ancient city going back at least 2,000 years. The rural areas were dotted with farming villages, often owned by wealthy landlords and worked by peasants, basically a feudal system.

It was a very interesting place to be stationed. In ancient times, Khuzestan had been the center of the Sassanid Empire (224-651CE) and a highly productive agricultural area. The nearby town of Susa had been the empire's capital, while Dezful had been a smaller settlement at one end of an ancient bridge over the Dez River, built by 70,000 captured Roman soldiers under Sassanid King Shahpur I in 260 AD. It is the oldest usable bridge in the world.[96] Thus, Dezful, or "Dezpul" in the local dialect, meant the Dez Bridge. Dezful was now the larger of the two towns, a bustling city of 130,000, while Susa was the much smaller historic site of Sassanid ruins.

Khuzestan Province was undergoing agricultural redevelopment, supported, in part, by the US government. Iranian and foreign companies were implementing large-scale irrigation schemes and modern farming techniques. The land was being leveled, and villages were being removed and consolidated into *shahraks*, small towns with government services, such as schools and clinics. It was a culturally diverse area, with Persians, Arabs, Luri, and Bakhtiari tribal people. The Dezful bazaar was also ancient and colorful, and the food was exotic and delicious.

The research station turned out to be a small building with minimal staff—one medical doctor, the director, one university-trained environmental engineer, three technicians, several high school graduate research assistants, and local laborers, about fifteen people in total. The objective of the research station was to conduct experiments and explore methods to control the snails that were the intermediate host of the waterborne parasitic disease, schistosomiasis, which was spreading through newly built irrigation canals. Schistosomiasis had been endemic in Khuzestan for hundreds of years. The research goal was to control or eliminate the reproduction of the snails that carried the parasite in water sources.

This job offered Paul his first opportunity to apply his newly acquired knowledge and skills in environmental engineering and explore a new persona, far from VMI cadet—that of a person with long hair and a full beard. His office colleagues told him he looked like a mullah, which they thought was an old-fashioned conservative look, while Paul felt he was finally keeping up with the times in America. He took up learning photography and spent hours photographing Iranian life and developing film in a darkroom he devised in the spare bedroom of our home. Because "ful" or "pul" in Persian means "bridge," as in "Dezpul" (Dez Bridge), Paul's new Iranian friends and colleagues thought Paul meant 'bridge' and called him "Mohandes Pul" or Engineer Bridge (or was it Bridge Engineer?). He fit right in.

The first challenge was communication, both in language and job description. First, very few colleagues spoke any English. Second, nobody could explain exactly what they expected Paul to do. When Paul arrived at the research station, the staff was occupied with applying a pesticide to irrigation canals to kill snails as part of a research project. Each day, the entire staff went to the field, leaving Paul behind because he wasn't part of that project. This continued for three months, leaving him unsure about his role. His job description had been vague. He was to be an adviser on environmental controls for schistosomiasis, but he also thought he would be absorbed into a team, which was not happening. He was replacing a previous adviser from the NEF but could not get an explanation of what he had done there. Perhaps his colleagues' silence on this subject was to allow time for Paul to adjust to the new culture, the research station, and its mission. Paul went out to look at villages with a driver and a non-English-speaking technician and tried to make sense of what he was supposed to do. While exploring solutions to the spread of schistosomiasis, Paul observed the way of life and learned about the local customs, beliefs, and Islam. We were invited to weddings, birth celebrations, and religious holidays and rituals. Through daily study and total immersion, both of us learned Farsi.

After three months, Paul decided he had to invent his job. At VMI, "Never say die." Never give up. Over the next several months, Paul identified three tasks the Ministry of Health could undertake. Snail-infested swampy areas needed to be drained, villages needed clean water systems, and specific canals needed immediate cleaning of vegetation and lining so the vegetation could not return. All of this would reduce the local population's contact with the parasite-contaminated water.

From this adventure in southern Iran, Paul learned that patience and perseverance—values learned at VMI and in his US Army assignments—are necessary complements to any professional or technical skills learned in college and graduate school. Iran had opened a new chapter in Paul's life. He was now sure that he wanted to see more of the world and continue to work in international development.

In late spring 1976, Paul's contract in Iran had ended, and I had concluded my research. We packed up a shipment of cultural artifacts and sent them to the US while we prepared to leave on a six-week journey home through Asia with my eighteen-year-old sister Marijo, who had joined us a few months earlier for a "gap year." On our last night in Iran, in the city of Ahwaz, while having dinner in a hotel, thieves broke into our car and stole all our luggage. All we had were the clothes on our backs, passports, and some cash. This is when we learned the art of traveling light. The three of us left on our trip with two plastic shopping bags containing toothbrushes and changes of underwear that we picked up on the way to the airport, and the next day bought a red canvas backpack from the Tehran Grand Bazaar. One of Paul's colleagues, in a gesture of friendship, met us at the Tehran airport with a parting gift—a large porcelain serving platter with a painted image of a turkey in the center. He said we could use it at Thanksgiving. It was not in a box or bag. The travel luggage now consisted of one backpack and a turkey platter! During our six-week trip, we visited India, Nepal, Thailand, Hong Kong, and Japan. Somewhere along the way, the turkey platter was donated.

Back in Chapel Hill, while I was writing my dissertation and waiting for our first baby, Paul enrolled in a PhD program at UNC. The World Bank was funding a project through the Department of Environmental Sciences and Engineering to use the power of the new microcomputers (IBM PC, Apple, Compaq) to streamline the planning and design of water and sanitation systems in developing countries. Up to this point, engineers had done planning and design by hand, which was extremely slow and inexact. Paul was part of the UNC project and preparing a dissertation on staged upgrading of water and sanitation systems in developing countries. Low-income communities could not afford sophisticated systems found in wealthier countries, so a staged approach might be the answer. Computers allowed for a quick comparison of different theoretical models. The World Bank and UNC wanted to demonstrate the practical application of these models.

The bank chose the Philippines, a World Bank loan recipient, to try out the concept. In 1981, they asked Paul if he could go there for a year or so to develop computer programs and train local staff in their use. Computers cut the time required to design a typical small urban system from several weeks to a few hours. Those trained would eventually train others in Asian countries (Bangladesh, China, Indonesia, Malaysia, Nepal, Pakistan, Sri Lanka, and Thailand). The family, now composed of three, moved to Quezon City, where a second child was born. The proposed one year ended up being over four years.

Having moved around so much, in 1985, we decided to create a home base in Steamboat Springs, Colorado. Paul had a contract with the World Bank for the next four years to continue his work in Asia, traveling out of Colorado. Remote work was barely heard of at that time. There was no Internet or email, but fax machines had just come on the market and served as the primary means of international communication, along with telephone calls and telex messages.

In January 1989, Paul accepted a one-year assignment with the Research Triangle Institute (under contract with UNDP/World Bank) to help Nepal develop a computerized database for water and sanitation systems throughout the country and identify those systems needing repair or upgrading. "Only about forty percent of the population had access to potable water and even less for sanitation," Paul explained. "Most of those systems were improved natural springs with piping to villages. Many of those systems were in disrepair. There was no database on the condition of these systems countrywide, nor the type of repairs needed." The project involved training government staff to use microcomputers for data management and analysis and surveying rural communities in the entire country with the help of the World Health Organization's local staff.

Soon after we arrived in Nepal, India slapped a commodities embargo on the country in retaliation for Nepal having purchased some defensive weapons from China. There was no gasoline or diesel, no food imports or commodities of any kind coming from India, Nepal's largest trading partner. With no vehicles on the roads, the highly polluted Kathmandu air cleared. We bought bicycles and ate whatever was in the market. Electricity came one to two hours per day, often in the middle of the night. We saved water in buckets when the taps flowed. The embargo lasted eleven months, and it turned out to be the best eleven months of our eventual eighteen-month stay—clear air, little noise, no traffic, a bicycling heaven. Our children attended the local international school, and Paul served as vice chair of the school board. We learned to speak a little Nepalese, took multiday treks, rode Nepalese ponies to nearby agricultural villages, visited the Chitwan National Park with its wild rhinos, elephants, and tigers, and learned a great deal about the culture.

However, the embargo delayed the Ministry's work. Staff could not get out to survey towns and villages due to lack of fuel. After India lifted the embargo, the World Bank extended Paul's contract for six months so the fieldwork could be carried out. The result was a Nepalese proposal to the World Bank for $10 million to repair and upgrade water systems around the country.

But that was not the entire adventure. A revolution to unseat the king took place in April 1990, when 200,000 people marched on the capital city of Kathmandu. They demanded the restoration of the Democratic multiparty system of government that had existed since 1950 but had slowly degraded into authoritarianism. Guns were fired, people were shot and killed, windows were broken, and statues were torn down. It lasted only a few days, with minimal loss of life. When the revolution ended, with an announcement by the king that he would restore a multiparty system, crowds swarmed the streets in celebration, handing out flowers to soldiers, putting red marks (*bindi*) on the foreheads of strangers, and throwing colored powder on each other. We joined in the celebration, one of several unforgettable moments of being in Nepal.

In January 1991, I began a position with the World Health Organization in Geneva in the Division of Environmental Health. After a few months of getting the family settled in Geneva, Paul began a new chapter in his career, serving as a senior desk officer for the UN's office for humanitarian relief in Iraq and the newly independent states of the former Soviet Union.

When US troops withdrew from Iraq at the end of the Gulf War in 1990, Iraq's President Sadam Hussein cut off food, medical supplies, and other commodities to Kurds in the north and Marsh Arabs and Shias in the south to subjugate them. These ethnic groups were struggling for independence from Iraq. Paul traveled with a UN team to Iraq to assess the need to raise international funds for relief.

After the fall of the Soviet Union in 1991, interethnic conflict in the former Soviet states resulted in population displacement, unemployment, and food insecurity. Homes and schools had no fuel for heating through terribly cold winters. Paul led assessments of humanitarian needs in some newly independent states, including Tajikistan, Georgia, Armenia, and Azerbaijan. Upon return to Geneva from these missions, Paul was responsible for coordinating international appeals for humanitarian relief.

All the while, beginning in 1991, Slobodan Milosevich, president of Yugoslavia, was waging war to "protect ethnic Serbs" from the newly self-declared independent states of Bosnia and Herzegovina and Croatia. Hundreds of thousands were displaced by conflict and ethnic cleansing carried out by the Serbian forces from 1991-1995. Paul became responsible for coordinating annual funding appeals for humanitarian relief for those displaced in the former Yugoslavia.

Following the intervention of the US and NATO forces in Bosnia in the fall of 1995 and the signing of the Dayton Peace Agreement in early 1996, the fighting ceased. In May 1996, the UN humanitarian agency asked Paul to go to Bosnia as an adviser to the UN refugee agency to assist in plans to resettle those displaced during the war. Paul spent eight months in Bosnia, witnessing the tragic devastation of Sarajevo and surrounding areas and the valiant efforts of Bosnians to reestablish their lives. He brought our two teenage children to Bosnia to work in brief internships with nonprofits, experiences that had a profound impact on their lives.

In mid-1998, Paul and I decided we needed a break. We resigned our positions in Geneva and returned to Steamboat Springs. To decompress from years of witnessing the horrors of wars, Paul took a job selling ski boots and teaching downhill skiing. But this did not last long. In the summer of 1999, the UN asked Paul to go to Albania to work with the Albanian government and the UN refugee agency to assist in the return of ethnic Albanian refugees from Kosovo. From 1991 to 1999, the conflicts in Yugoslavia had displaced about 800,000 people, and many of those had fled to Albania. In 1999, NATO bombed Serbia to end the conflict.

With so many Yugoslavians displaced from the Balkan Wars, in the autumn of 2000, the UN asked Paul to lead its country office of humanitarian affairs in Belgrade, Serbia. His mission was to coordinate UN and nongovernmental humanitarian relief for the returning displaced persons, many of whom were ethnic "Roma" and other non-Serb minorities. In Belgrade, shops that had been closed for months or years were starting to reopen. People were friendly but also still reeling from the NATO bombing in mid-1999. Serbs had mixed feelings about Americans. I joined him in May 2001 and later taught at the University of Belgrade as a Fulbright Scholar.

While in Belgrade, Paul had been attending a local Rotary Club, as he was already a Rotarian in Steamboat Springs. Before he left for a Christmas break in 2000, the Belgrade Rotary Club told Paul that they had a request from social services for warm jackets for refugees living in temporary quarters, such as schools and other public buildings. It was winter, and it was cold. Paul said he would see what he could do. Upon arriving in Steamboat Springs, he put out a call to the Steamboat Springs Rotary Club and other friends and collected about fifty warm winter jackets that he carried back to Belgrade as excess baggage.

While Paul was in Serbia, a great famine had developed in Ethiopia. The UN asked Paul to move to Ethiopia to head the office and continue coordinating food and other relief. Some 13 million people were food insecure, and many children were dying of starvation. Ethiopia has a history of famines, with the 1984 famine being one of the most famous, caused by drought, war, and military policies intended to weaken political rivals. Once again, Ethiopia had starvation in the south and east of the country, this time caused by severe drought and a lack of emergency food stockpiles. Paul traveled the country to witness the needs and oversaw studies of the Ethiopian government's efforts to improve agriculture to prevent future famines. Some of the challenges he faced in Ethiopia were the fact that agencies don't like to be coordinated, and governments don't like to see reports that aren't favorable. The Ethiopian government was not always pleased with the work of his office. As Paul rose to take on more challenging roles, the leadership traits learned at VMI and in the Army came into focus.

In 2007, the UN asked Paul to lead an investigative mission into the humanitarian needs in a war zone in eastern Ethiopia. Those needs were food, medical assistance, shelter, security, and drinking water. In addition, the military was preventing traditional livestock trade across the border with Somalia, which was the main source of livelihood.

Ethiopia has several ethnic groups, each with its own language and culture, and each longing for autonomy or dominance. The current national government was led by one such group, the Tigrayan National Liberation Front, which had overthrown the previous communist government. Sensitivities among the groups were high, and one group or another was always vying for power. One of those was the Ogaden National Liberation Front (ONLF), which, since 1994, had been leading an insurgency in the Somali Region of Ethiopia for social and political autonomy from the central government. (The Ogaden people are a clan of Ethiopian Somali people.) The Ethiopian government had conducted counterinsurgency measures that had resulted in reported atrocities. In the summer of 2007, the government was responding to an attack by the ONLF on a Chinese oil exploration camp, where some twenty Chinese and several Ethiopian soldiers had been killed. Reports were coming in that the military was blocking food aid to villages, preventing traditional livestock trading and access to water sources, apparently aimed at groups supporting the ONLF. People were suffering. "The government objected to the mission because they said it was too dangerous, but they just did not want the UN to see what the military was doing to the local population," Paul said.

"The morning of the mission, I learned that the night before, the drivers of our ten vehicles had been warned by the governor of the Somali Region that, if they drove the vehicles, there would be some serious consequences. I assured them that we would protect them, and the UN would stand by them," he said. The government continued to put up obstacles to the mission, assigning a TV network to film, warning villagers not to say anything negative, assigning a military escort, and arresting and jailing people who talked to them. In the end, while the government allowed the UN to give humanitarian relief to the population, they indicated that they were not pleased with the final report from the mission, especially regarding the human rights abuses, and refused to let that portion remain in the report.

By late 2007, Paul realized he had used up his goodwill with the government of Ethiopia and requested a transfer to Nairobi, Kenya, where I was based with Catholic Relief Services. The UN humanitarian office there was responding to election violence and population displacement. This move to Nairobi led to a new, rewarding experience in education philanthropy. A Rotary Club in Denver, Colorado, learned that Paul was in Nairobi and asked him to join a small team from their club to visit a private primary school for orphans they were supporting, located on the outskirts of Nairobi's largest informal settlement, Kibera. The club needed someone to handle tuition money to support twenty high school students who had graduated from primary school. They were hoping Paul would agree. Most high schools in Kenya are private boarding schools, and these orphans did not have families who could pay. After visiting the 350-student school, the inevitable happened. Paul agreed to be a conduit for the funds, and we became active supporters of the school.

The school buildings were constructed of sheet metal, and the library was in a metal shipping container. The external walls of the buildings were delightfully painted with images of African animals. Lunch for the children—a mixture of maize and beans flavored with onion and tomato—was cooked in one giant pot on a wood fire supported by three stones. It took about twelve hours to prepare lunch for these children and used a great deal of wood. Paul raised funds from friends and colleagues in the US and Switzerland to build additional classrooms from concrete blocks, construct a fuel-efficient wood-burning stove to replace their "three-stone" cooking method, and sponsor several more children to high school. One donor contracted a professional fundraising video. Paul provided financial accounting for the funds until 2013.

Paul retired from the UN in mid-2008 and for the next three years, he worked out of Nairobi as a consultant to various humanitarian organizations in East Africa, conducting evaluations of past projects.

In 2010, VMI caught up with Paul through Facebook, sending him a message that they had selected him to receive the 2011 Jonathan Daniels '61 Humanitarian Award. "I thought it was a joke or spam," Paul said, "because I had only been in contact with a few brother rats over the years. Receiving the award was an unexpected thrill. VMI prepared me for my international journey and taught me many of the lessons I needed to pursue the work and life that I chose," he said. He contributed the $25,000 award money to the primary school in Kenya.

We retired at the end of 2010 and returned home to Colorado. By this time, Paul had worked and lived in eleven countries and worked in an additional thirteen. Our dreams of having an international life had come true. Paul summarized his life by saying, "I could have chosen a different path, an easier path, working as an engineer for a big corporation like Bechtel, but it is not what I wanted to do."

In 2013, VMI invited Paul to share his career experience as a visiting professor in the International Studies Program. He then returned to teach again in 2015. In 2017, 2018, and 2019, VMI invited him to teach environmental science in the Civil and Environmental Engineering Department, the same department that had taught him fifty years earlier, where he developed a curriculum minor in environmental studies. As a professor, he said that he gained a new perspective on the Institute and cadets.

> "I was impressed by the positive changes at VMI since I was a cadet there. Now there were Black students, female students, and a greatly expanded curriculum. One of the best additions to their education is the chance to have a semester abroad. I was also impressed with the maturity of the young men and women in my classes. They had a broader understanding of world events than I had as a cadet. I loved coming back to the Institute as a teacher."

After the murder of George Floyd that rocked the nation, Paul supported the removal of Confederate and Civil War symbols from VMI, including the removal of the statue of Confederate General Thomas Jackson from the head of the parade ground. He conveyed his thoughts to the superintendent and the president of the BOV. He engaged in a lot of email "talk" among his brother rats, who seemed to be divided on attitudes toward change at the Institute. Some were for VMI moving out of the Civil War sentimentality and putting all those Confederate symbols in a museum, and others were for retaining all the VMI traditions that glorified VMI's role in the Civil War. "The emails were quite contentious, and I was frankly shocked by many of the things some of my brother rats wrote. But I am so glad VMI has decided mostly to put the Civil War in the past and move into the modern era of inclusiveness." He feels that General Wins was a great choice to move VMI forward.

LOOKING BACK

Reflecting on his education at VMI, Paul said he received a solid engineering education and the strength to endure some of the challenges he faced in his career, especially enduring difficult work conditions in crises. He felt the VMI Honor Code served him well in building trust with national counterparts in various countries. "It took me forty years to appreciate how much VMI had taught me, had toughened me, and had disciplined me." He feels that the "drumming out" ceremony is "over-the-top" and should be eliminated. He said he still remembers how "chilling" it was to see someone drummed out. "It would be just enough to be expelled," he said.

"With the changes since 1968, I believe VMI has a bright future," Paul said. "The Institute has essentially fulfilled the dreams of VMI's founders. VMI has moved far beyond what the founders could have even imagined."

Paul Hebert was not the only '68 graduate to pursue an international humanitarian career. His brother rat, Robert

Macpherson, following service as an infantry officer in the Marines and retiring as a colonel, embarked on a second career with the humanitarian organization CARE, where he led humanitarian response missions worldwide. He relates the highlights of his second career in his book, *Stewards of Humanity*, published in 2021.[97]

CLASS OF '68 ADVICE TO THE INSTITUTE

★ ★ ★

"Continue to make VMI unique and stress that the Honor Code is a life code, and mottoes like on our ring 'Honor Above Self' will serve VMI men and women their entire lives."
—A graduate, Class of '68

VMI has a strong alumni association that strives to stay in close contact with graduates through a quarterly publication called *The Alumni Review* and through class reunions every five years. The VMI communications department puts out a monthly newsletter, *The Institute Report*, that is sent to every graduate with an address known to VMI. VMI holds several ceremonial events during the academic year, as well as football and basketball games, that draw graduates back to the Institute. VMI graduates, therefore, have every opportunity to keep up with VMI news and changes. As a result, it seemed this book would not be complete without asking these graduates whether they had some advice for the Institute.

The advice compiled here was offered in response to questions in the 2018 survey. Many changes took place at VMI between 2019 and 2022, including the removal of the Jackson statue and the creation of a new Office of Diversity, Opportunity and Inclusion. While these are burning issues today, they were not when I sent out this survey, and thus, for better or worse, we do not have these graduates' opinions on these topics.

While VMI has made several changes over the past fifty years, much about the college and its ROTC program remains the same. It is that sameness that many graduates appreciate the most—the preservation of traditions that they believe produce graduates of integrity. More than half of the men said they were happy with the changes that VMI has already made, such as admitting women and having greater racial diversity in the Cadet Corps. Many said that VMI is better now than fifty years ago:

"I believe that today's graduates are much better prepared for life than I was in 1968. I must say, from all I've observed at VMI over the last fifty years, I'm impressed in all areas."

"Actually, I think VMI is great just as it is now. So much better than when I was a cadet."

"From what I've seen and read about VMI, it is doing a great job in all areas."

"I am extremely impressed with all aspects of VMI's proactive approach to improving curriculum, cadet life, and training for life after VMI. My advice? Keep doing what you're doing!"

Looking back on their own lives, several praised the Institute for a job well done, saying, "VMI toughened me up and made me feel like I could handle any challenge, overcome any obstacle, and handle extreme pressure. I am extremely grateful for my VMI experience, and it has served me very well."

But, in addition to praise, eighty-five men had suggestions for VMI largely centered around helping cadets to mature and be ready to take on life's challenges. Their advice fell into five areas.

TEACH CADETS "LIFE 101"

Several men said that they had been woefully unprepared for life when they came to VMI and when they left. They complained of being naïve and immature and not knowing much of anything about women, marriage, parenting, finances, investments, insurance, how to rent an apartment, and other life challenges. So, they offered some ideas.

A couple of men said they knew nothing about girls when they entered VMI—and nothing when they left! One man said he didn't know how to dance. One man suggested offering a course called "Life 101" that would include how to choose a marriage partner, how to keep a marriage going, and how to be a parent.

"Marriage and parenting are the two most important things we need to do very well, but there is little training anywhere in our society for these."

Others said cadets should be taught how to live on their own in an apartment, how to manage finances, how to choose a health insurance plan, and how to make investments and save for retirement. One wrote, "A condensed course on finance and investment would be invaluable for all cadets as they pursue their chosen careers." They said it would be great if the Institute could find a way to teach these basic life skills.

Similarly, some men suggested that cadets be more exposed to the real world:

"More social interaction outside the confines of the Institute."

"Require cadets to intern in public or community service during free summers. Offer off-post volunteer opportunities during the school year. Offer a broad course of study on the environment and cultures of the world."

One suggested providing "whatever it takes to transport students to other parts of Virginia. Having no car inhibits their education. Especially all students from out of state."

In a similar vein, several said that VMI was a bit too isolated and restrictive on social life, that VMI should give cadets more freedom and provide more opportunities for social life. Some said that because VMI has admitted women, the male cadets will be better prepared for relationships with women. One also said that perhaps VMI should allow some limited use of alcohol or classes on responsible use of alcohol, as making it off-limits causes folks to want it more.

IMPROVE ACADEMIC AND CAREER COUNSELING

Several men suggested improving academic and career counseling based on their own experiences of not being very good students when they were at VMI:

"Simply assigning a faculty member to advise as an additional duty, with no formal training in advising, was inadequate."

"Faculty advisers need to recognize cadets who are 'sliding' academically and ensure they are helped. In some cases, this may mean being insistent, even when the cadet resists being helped. Equally, cadets should realize when they need help; [they should] overcome their pride and seek help and insist that they get it."

"I know that I was a very poor student academically and very reluctant to seek help. I didn't know how to study, and so that part of VMI was constant drudgery and never really fun. And so, my 'advice' is not really that, but instead, a question. Is there a mechanism, a process of sorts, a safety net, that would identify the dumbasses like me early on and point them (with due pressure) in the direction of counselors and tutors that I know are available to cadets?"

"I failed the Institute and myself because of my immaturity, but if I could turn back time, I would want some official someone to take enough interest to help me get it right."

"I would have liked to have had a better adviser to encourage me."

"Put more of your best, most relatable instructors in rat classes. The better the start—the stronger the finish."

TEACH BUSINESS SKILLS

Teaching business skills was another suggestion offered by several graduates.

> Require business classes so that any cadet entering the business world understands money flow and being able to run a business. Almost become a CPA. Finances and business

budgeting are extremely important and should be taught at the undergraduate level. Bring in alumni to discuss these topics at the basic level, which is what the cadet will face after graduation. Money matters, insurance, savings, and stock market activities should be presented in curriculum studies. Household budgeting may sound simple, but when out on your own and newly married, it becomes a challenge.

"I would make a class on finance mandatory... everything from managing a checking account to financing a house. Manage credit cards, investments, retirement accounts."

I think all majors should be required to take a general business course (four semesters) that covers introductions to finance, accounting, business law, and strategic planning. It should also provide some comparative analysis of the superiority of free enterprise capitalism to other economic structures. Regardless of career path, military, or private sector, this is fundamental knowledge that will benefit for a lifetime.

"International and business studies are a big plus."
"Economics and accounting for basic understanding of business."

VMI is isolated from the business world. I'd like to see much more training for what a graduate will encounter in the real world of business, the cutthroat stuff... all that crap that is unknown to a VMI graduate. Role-playing or videos of office scenarios would be incredibly useful. I'd also like to see salesmanship techniques taught since sales techniques are used by everyone, even non-salesmen, to get what they want. Straight-commission sales professionals should teach sales techniques.

In a similar vein, one man wrote, "If you leave VMI and enter the military as an officer, you will be entering a highly structured environment where you do your job and never make your superior officer look bad. If you leave VMI and enter the business world, you'll have to work your way up the ladder, and it's dog-eat-dog all the way. Both should be taught at VMI."

STRENGTHEN CERTAIN COURSE AREAS

Several men felt that VMI should strengthen certain academic courses. One said that VMI should emphasize history, the US Constitution, the value of a civil society, and capitalism. A few others said that all students should be required to take courses in international studies. Several emphasized that VMI graduates should have strong communication skills:

"What sets people apart the most in the workplace is the ability to speak and write clearly. I would suggest a continued emphasis on critical thinking and its importance to clear and effective communications."

"Academic/technical education is important, and you will have to continue development in technical training through a career, but even more important are communication and interpersonal skills."

Others added that VMI cadets should be educated and prepared for specific jobs. Some men suggested that the cadets have opportunities for internships and job experience before graduation. "Developing a cooperative program with industries so that students can build a résumé of experience and academic accomplishment would enhance job offers at graduation."

TEACH ETHICS FOR THE REAL WORLD

Two men said that, when they were cadets, VMI did not teach them that not all people have the same understanding of integrity that a VMI graduate has and that VMI graduates will encounter dishonest people but not be able to recognize them.

"Make sure cadets understand that most people will not have the same standards that VMI graduates live by."

"A course on ethics—reflecting the real world outside of VMI—would have value. VMI's Honor Code carries forward as a major tenet of success for alumni. Ethics in today's world is a challenge, and graduates should be aware that colleagues in all professions do not share the same code of conduct."

"Teach students to be open-minded but dedicated to ethical behavior."

Above all, the one suggestion repeated most often was that VMI should continue to stress the value of the VMI Honor Code in creating honest, trustworthy individuals for our society.

AFTERWORD

★ ★ ★

"Writing a book is an adventure. To begin with it is a toy, then an amusement. Then it becomes a mistress, and then it becomes a master, and then it becomes a tyrant and, in the last stage, just as you are about to be reconciled to your servitude, you kill the monster and fling him to the public."
—Winston Churchill

This book began as a small project to document the lives and values of the VMI Class of 1968 and their advice to future cadets and the Institute.

My plan was to take a scientific approach: send out a questionnaire and summarize the results. I had three simple questions: Wouldn't it be interesting to know what happened to the Class of 1968? Would those cadets who marched in the parade for the fiftieth reunion of the Class of 1968 be interested in what happened to that class? And did the Class of 1968 fulfill the founder's intentions to produce men of honor and integrity and citizen-soldiers?

I thought it would be a simple task to collate the answers and produce the findings for posterity. *No big deal*, I thought. *A simple project. I will finish within a year.*

But, as Churchill said in the quote above, the book became a master, then a tyrant. I soon realized, in trying to present answers to these questions, I had to explain VMI, its history, its traditions, and its methods of training and educating its students. That raised many more questions as to why VMI was founded, how it got involved in the Civil War, and how that legacy stayed with VMI to almost the present moment. Then I had to explain myself because I had not grown up in the South, and I saw VMI through a Yankee's eyes. This resulted in a much longer book than I had anticipated and took much more time. I ended up spending four years writing this book! But, following that journey, here are some further conclusions and observations.

First, yes, the VMI Class of 1968 did fulfill the founder's intentions and dreams. The men's responses showed that VMI's educational system, and especially the Honor Code, had made a huge impression on their lives. They mentioned honor over and over in their responses. These men who responded to the survey said that they followed the VMI Honor Code in their lives. When they strayed, the result was negative. They support VMI's single-sanction system that reinforces the message that being honorable and having integrity is essential, not only for our military but for success in life in general.

VMI has kept its military-style educational system with few changes through the Class of 1968 and up to today due to steady leadership from superintendents who graduated from VMI. Thirteen of the sixteen superintendents, since founding, were VMI graduates, and the other three graduated from US Military Academies at West Point and Annapolis. What I think makes VMI unique is its strong emphasis on honor, discipline, and brotherhood, a combination not necessarily found in other colleges.

Of the main reasons VMI was founded—to strengthen the Virginia militia through the creation of citizen-soldiers, fears of slave uprisings, the desire to extend the right to vote to all White males in the state, regardless of landholding status, and a need for engineers in the state—I conclude that all four reasons were important. Some may have been more important than others to certain individuals. Clearly, Preston was focused on creating citizen-soldiers and higher education for young men who were not the sons of wealthy landowners, replacing rowdy militiamen who had become the "... undesirable element in the quiet community of Scots-Irish Presbyterians" in Lexington.[98] Crozet felt strongly about the need for Virginia to train engineers, and he appreciated a military-style education. Lexington shop owner Barclay was impressed by his visit to the US Military Academy at West Point and could envision a similar academy for the state of Virginia. Smith, an academic, was also likely to favor a military-style education as a graduate of West Point. And probably at the back of everyone's mind was this question of slavery and abolition, and who would be ready to defend Virginia's population in the event of a slave uprising? Who would put down an uprising? It would be the Virginia militia, a loosely organized set of officers, mainly plantation owners, scattered across the state, some of whom had trained at West Point, headed by the state governor. Perhaps VMI could offer a steady flow of well-trained young men across the state who could respond quickly to any state emergency or foreign invasion with military leadership. We can imagine these four founders, and perhaps others, sitting around Preston's dining table in 1836, planning a new military institute at the arsenal that would fulfill all these needs and bring greater development to western Virginia. It was an experiment, and it worked. The purpose of VMI has expanded over the years and goes beyond the ideas of the founders while its essential elements have remained intact. Today, VMI is national and international in focus, producing reserve officers for all military branches and graduates outstanding in their respective fields.

One could ask why college students still choose to enroll in a military college like VMI, The Citadel, or federal military colleges like the United States Military Academy at West Point. These colleges are not easy. Creigh Kelley, Class of '68, said that VMI was more difficult than being in Vietnam. My answer, and I may be wrong, is that the young people who apply do not fully realize what they are getting into. And how could they? Few know the history of VMI or even why VMI continues to exist today. They are going because of family tradition, a sports scholarship, someone recommended they apply, or VMI's excellent academic program. Fair enough. VMI has had an excellent reputation in Virginia. Ninety-eight percent of VMI graduates land good jobs or are admitted to graduate programs soon after graduation. Few new cadets anticipate spending their lives as military officers, and few ever do have military careers. In the Class of '68, only fifteen did so. Yet the lure of a military-style education endures. Today, many serve as officers in one of the military branches.

The history of VMI shows how institutions change as society changes. Some respond more quickly to societal changes, while others change more slowly or reluctantly. VMI changed slowly and reluctantly when admitting Black students, enrolling women, and facing its Confederate image. I believe VMI changed slowly because its BOV and alumni believed so deeply in its traditions. For 129 years, they believed that the educational system offered by VMI was only appropriate for White males, and for 167 years, they believed VMI was appropriate only for males. VMI had a very hard time realizing that it was a White patriarchal institution. In fact, for most of its history, VMI leadership, faculty, or alumni would have never used those terms. One VMI graduate of that era told me that students back then didn't see the lack of diversity as an issue. But of course, we did have on blinders, just as Longwood College, my alma mater in Farmville, Virginia, was for White females only. I remember, in those days, that Longwood had a culture of silence around racial issues. So, it must have been at VMI. Those were the societal values of White Virginians at the time VMI was founded and remained so almost until the turn of the twenty-first century. Until the 1970s, most Virginia colleges were still segregated by gender and race. VMI was among the very last colleges in the nation to admit Black students, having little choice after the 1964 Civil Rights Acts, the last state-supported college to admit women after a Supreme Court decision. We can look back and see this history, and then we move forward. We now see diversity and inclusion as traits that make education stronger, just as these men in the Class of '68 have advised.

VMI still has a challenge with the lack of diversity. Only about 6 percent of the student body has an African American heritage, about 12 to 14 percent are women, and over the years, VMI has had very few Indigenous students (although there is no firm data available on Indigenous students). There are three in the Class of 2024.

Something else interesting to note is that VMI has welcomed foreign students for more than 100 years. The first foreign student, a young man from China, was admitted in 1903. VMI had at least two more Chinese students from China, General Hsi Kuei Tseng, who graduated in 1925, and General Sun Li-Yen, who graduated in 1927. VMI has had scores of Thai students, at least one from Singapore, about forty or more from Iran in the 1970s, one or more from Germany, and in recent years, one from Kenya. VMI has alumni associations in Korea, Europe, Taiwan, and Thailand. Many members may be American citizens stationed abroad, but each of these associations has nationals who attended VMI. The Thai chapter has 100 members. VMI's Alumni Association and VMI Archives has no compiled data on its foreign students beyond the Chinese student of 1903.[99] I only learned about these foreign students from alumni who remember them in their classes, anecdotal information from Todd Goen, director of international students at VMI, and the VMI Archives. In researching this book, I was surprised to learn that eastern Virginia's wealthy plantation owners, such as the Cocke family, the Wise family, and the Ruffins, were drawn to VMI from the earliest days. They sent their sons to the Institute for generations, and they provided funds and other support.

While I conclude this book, VMI is still going through changes to encourage more students of various backgrounds to become cadets. In closing, my hope is that this book has captured the spirit of VMI, its secret sauce, how it challenges cadets, shapes lives, and produces leaders that our country needs.

REMARKS TO THE FIFTIETH REUNION

* ★ *

CLASS OF 1968, 20 APRIL 2018— GENERAL J. H. BINFORD PEAY, III SUPERINTENDENT

The following speech has only been edited for capitalizations and punctuation.

Members of the VMI class of 1968, spouses, and friends. Good evening, and welcome back to VMI. Since graduating from the Institute, many of you have returned to celebrate class reunions five, ten, and twenty-five years out, but surely nothing can compare with returning for your fiftieth reunion. This anniversary comes at a time when most of you have achieved the high goals that you set for yourselves in those formative days here at VMI. And even now, new goals and adventures beckon you forward. This is a special moment, and the Institute and I feel very privileged to share it with you.

Every year that marks the graduation of a class at VMI is special, but 1968 was more than special: *it was an extraordinary time.* TIME magazine described it as: "War Abroad, Riots at Home, Fallen Leaders, and Lunar Dreams: The Year that Changed the World." It was a turning point not only in American history but across the globe. Countless books and studies have been written about the year 1968, and I believe historians will continue to focus on this period for decades to come.

Developments in world affairs, science, and society were bringing about fundamental changes and setting new directions for the future. Two years before you entered VMI, Colonel John H. Glenn Jr. became the first US astronaut to orbit the Earth. During that year, James D. Watson, Frances Crick, and Maurice Wilkins received the Nobel Prize for the discovery of the molecular structure of DNA. In the spring, United States forces were ordered to Laos, and President Kennedy announced that US advisers in Vietnam would fire if fired upon. In September of 1962, the US Circuit Court ordered the University of Mississippi to admit African American student James H. Meredith. One month later, President Kennedy announced that the Soviet Union was building offensive weapons bases in Cuba and ordered a naval and air quarantine of offensive military equipment. Conflict was avoided when Russia agreed to halt construction, dismantle, and remove its rockets, and a long but difficult Cold War began. The following year, 1963, saw a worsening of the conflict in Vietnam, and the Civil Rights Movement accelerated under the guidance of Dr. Martin Luther King Jr., who delivered his "I Have a Dream Speech" in August. In November, the nation was shocked by the assassination of President Kennedy, and upon his death, Vice President Lyndon B. Johnson became president.

In the months before you matriculated, which included the lead-up to the next presidential election, the nation saw the first draft-card burning demonstrations as opposition to the US involvement in Vietnam grew. While civil rights activists were being murdered in the South, President Johnson signed the Civil Rights Act of 1964. The following year, VMI's own Jonathan Daniels would lose his life for that cause.

This was the backdrop to your arrival at the Institute.

As I researched your class in the VMI archive records, conversed with retired administrators and instructors, and scoured your very dedicated class agent's reports and articles, an interesting picture and proud history emerged.

It has been fifty-four years since 368 of you signed the Matriculation Book and became VMI cadets. The day was the 10th of September 1964, and it marked the beginning of VMI's 125th year. On that day, you started a five-day "New Cadet Orientation and Training Period," better known as Cadre, which a writer in the VMI CADET described by saying, "thus began the long difficult process of learning and living the VMI way of life." For most the rest of the year, you were known to the upper classes as "the rat mass." It would be some very long months of testing, and not until nearly the end of the academic year did you become "the fourth class," the "class of 1968."

Not only was your class the largest entering class in VMI history, up to that time, but for the first time in years, the majority of the class initially majored in scientific or technical fields.

The barracks that you entered were much like today's barracks, although it consisted only of Old and New Barracks. New Barracks had been completed fifteen years before, and the north end had been reserved for administrative offices, including the superintendent's office and rooms for the VMI Board of Visitors. Because of growing enrollment and overcrowding, these administrative offices were turned into cadet rooms, and administrators prepared to move to the new Smith Hall and Lejeune Hall, then planned and under construction.

Life at VMI was conducted under the watchful eye of commandant of cadets, Colonel George H. Simpson, '40, until 1966, when he was succeeded "in turn" by Colonel William J. Boehmer, '42 (who died in his first month), Col. Lloyd L. Leech Jr., '42, who was soon promoted to brigadier general and shortly transferred, and Colonel Douglas C. France Jr., '41, who served until 1970. The superintendent, who had been appointed my second class year, in 1960, was Brigadier General George R. E. Shell, '31, and he served in that post throughout your cadetship.

After being introduced to the Rat Line, the upper class leadership and the rat disciplinary committee issued a warning to you that they had started a "campaign" to regain the class system and Rat Line which, they said, had been "relaxed" over the past several years. Soon, a daily routine developed of classes, exams, military duty, and the normal life of a cadet. This was relieved from time to time by Parents Weekend, athletic events, special lectures, formal dances, trips to the fifth stoop, and spring hike. Some of you joined the "Wednesday and Saturday Gun and Hiking Club," another name for penalty tours. And there were ceremonies, especially the impressive New Market Ceremony during which Senator Harry F. Byrd received the cherished New Market Medal. Shortly before that ceremony, Breakout arrived, and you officially became a class. Whereupon, you elected Joseph Addison Hagan, III, president, John Joseph Ramsburg, vice-president, and Joe Oliver Smith, historian. Later, Smith was elected vice president, and William Preston Boyer Jr. was elected historian. On 13 June 1965, Colonel John H. Glenn Jr. delivered the graduation address, in front of Preston Library, and your first year was over.

During your third class year, 1965-1966, which some have described generally as the year of "the academic Rat Line," VMI continued to grow. Another record number of new cadets matriculated, and the faculty was expanded.

In January 1966, the corps, at full strength, marched in the inaugural parade of Governor Mills E. Godwin Jr. The corps was greeted in Richmond with a blanket of snow and sub-freezing temperatures. A month later, a blizzard hit Lexington, with over two feet of snow, stranding cadets who were attempting to leave on semester break.

Governor Godwin was the commencement speaker on 12 June 1966. General Shell was superintendent, and the dean of the faculty was the highly respected James M. Morgan, Jr. . . . Both Shell and Morgan Halls are named today in their honor.

The archives reveal that your second class year, 1966-1967, brought to a head a number of disagreements between the corps and the administration over the activities of the Honor Court and general committee, furlough, late study, administration of the Rat

Line, and cadet privileges. This led to the unprecedented decision of the class of 1967, with support from your class and the rest of the corps, to threaten a boycott of the Thanksgiving game with Virginia Tech in Roanoke.

Despite the controversy, Ring Figure came, with its party in the Pine Room. Your historian summed up the following days of the "Dark Ages": "The long winter of everyone's discontent roared in and settled down with us until Spring Vacation. Mid-Winter provided a needed lift of spirits as once again dates appeared, music was heard, [and] smiles were seen . . ." Another improvement for Cadet life was the completion and opening of the new corps building, Lejeune Hall. The new building enabled an expansion of extra-curricular activities, headed by a director of cadet affairs, Col. Flournoy Barksdale, '40. The facility contained a book store, a new PX, a bowling alley, a large activities room, and—most importantly—a "tube room" where cadets could watch a television set. Having access to this television proved increasingly important as events in the nation became increasingly troublesome and even violent.

Across the nation, campus unrest was growing, now with special emphasis on opposition to the draft. Large demonstrations were held in New York City and San Francisco. This was closely watched by VMI cadets and writers for the VMI CADET. Also watched closely was the six-day war as Israel launched a preemptive strike against Egyptian Air Force airfields, drawing in Syria and Iraq. By the 10th of June, the war ended with a cease-fire. The speaker at June graduation, 1967, was General Earle G. Wheeler, chairman of the Joint Chiefs of Staff . . . culminating your second class year.

Your first class year, 1967-1968, from my perspective, was eventful.

It started off pretty much as the previous three years had begun. A large rat class was inducted into the VMI way of life by Van Landingham, president of the Honor Court; Hagan, class and general committee president, and Joe Smith, your first captain.

Yet, a "simmering dissatisfaction" over the perceived weakening of the class system and the Rat Line continued throughout the year. Interesting, that friction continues to this day. The problem was seen as a conflict with the administration and also as a conflict with the academic program. On the national level, there was a similar conflict between the military action in Vietnam and the goals of the Johnson administration's "Great Society." In October, the massive "March on Washington" took place. A November piece in *the CADET* reveals the depth of that concern. It stated, "Is the present escalation policy the correct course for the United States in Vietnam? Pragmatically, it cannot be supported because those who carry out the policy of escalation see the problem of Vietnam as a military problem. So while we are winning a military engagement we are not achieving our political goals of peace negotiation or the cessation of infiltration of supplies and men from North to South Vietnam." *The CADET* also reported on 2 February 1968 on the capture of the US Naval intelligence ship, PUEBLO, by North Korea. Officials in Washington called this "a functional equivalent" of a declaration of war. In the same issue was the first report of the death of an alumnus in Vietnam, the first of five or six before your class graduated. Such news, as today, was announced at SRC with a moment of silence and by the flying of the American flag at half staff in front of barracks, a sad reminder that was increasingly to be seen over the next several years. Furthermore, tactical officers began to be called away to serve in Vietnam, and new TAC officers arrived who had served there, bringing the war even closer to the Institute. The great football victory . . . 12 to 10 . . . over VA Tech on Thanksgiving brought enormous satisfaction to the corps and alumni . . . particularly after the drubbing the previous year.

In February 1968, it was reported that VMI had accepted its first Black cadet, and that four others were also being evaluated for admission. The next year, 1968-69, would see the first Black cadets enrolled at VMI. The admission of women, however, would wait for another thirty years.

Some profound shocks to the nation were soon to come. President Johnson announced that he would not run for reelection... and in early April, Dr. Martin Luther King was assassinated in Memphis. In mid-May, the US and North Vietnam entered into peace talks in Paris, a hopeful sign according to most cadets.

Your graduation took place in front of Preston Library on the 7th of June, 1968. The highly respected Judge J. Randolph Tucker Jr., '35, delivered the commencement address. The first Jackson-Hope went to George Hubert ("Skip") Roberts Jr.; the second Jackson-Hope went to Kenneth James Perkins, and the Cincinnati Medal went to Guy Alpheus Wilson. Your historian concluded his class essay in the 1968 BOMB with these words: "When we gaze at the VMI diploma in later years, most of us will be able to realize that what we went through as cadets was indeed valuable. The Rat Line and its demands will seem paltry when compared to the tasks that will be assigned. The long hours of work, the sacrifices of personal pride in favor of a greater ideal, and the necessity of working with individuals of different talents and states of mind are not met only here at VMI. Life outside is much more demanding, but we now may rest secure in our experience."

A wonderful and timeless message.

And how did the class of 1968 meet the challenges of life "outside"? What a record you have achieved since those cadet days. I confess these results... made more difficult as some of you have had several professions... are my quick unscientific study of your accomplishments: 111 of you became businessmen, managers, or CEOs; 29 entered the legal profession; 28 became physicians; 20 became educators; 18 entered finance and government service; 17 were engineers; 15 made the military a career; 6 entered law enforcement; 5 became scientists; 4 became contractors; 3 became writers or journalists and pilots; 2 became farmers, artists, or clergymen. Of your class, 215 served in the armed forces, with 142 in the Army, 56 in the Air Force, 12 in the Marine Corps, 4 in the Navy, and one in the Coast Guard. Impressively, your class has served the Institute in large numbers with McDowell on the Board of Visitors; Philpott, Jeffress and Barton as presidents of the VMI Foundation further supported with Gibbons, Boyd, and Holland; and Donald, Kevin Henry, Kemper, Hickey, and Holland serving on the Keydet Club. Jim Henry serves on the Alumni Association . . . Steve Wilson has been the Army PMS and detachment commander and Paul Hebert awarded the Daniels Award and currently teaching here, and Farmer, Bowers, and Martin have been or are chapter presidents or representatives. Certainly, Skip Roberts's executive leadership of the foundation and his legal support to many entities has been so valuable. And on a very personal note . . . my close friend from childhood days, Senator Tom Norment, has been invaluable to the attainment of goals and success of Vision 2039 while serving the commonwealth with great leadership and strength. . . . He deserves enormous credit for the state of the Institute today. This is an outstanding record for a VMI class, and this evening I want to acknowledge your contributions to the Institute, to our state, and to the nation. Congratulations!

But let us not spend our entire evening just looking back. Reunion is also a time to "reconnect" with today's Institute . . . learning about where the Institute is today and where it is heading.

Like most VMI alumni, whenever I think about today's Institute—which by many measures is fulfilling its historic mission well beyond the dreams of our founders—I think about where we have been and where we may be heading. To recount all the significant events and turning points that have occurred in the life of VMI since its founding in 1839 would be interesting and inspiring, but such a review would demand more time than we have this evening. Instead, I need only look back a half century—to your graduation—to suggest, with a few examples, how things have changed . . . and, yet, how much has stayed the same.

Fifty years ago, the Corps of Cadets numbered a little over 1,000; today it began academic year 2017-18 at 1,726 cadets. In part, this growth has been made possible by the addition of a new barracks—the third in the line of historic buildings that make up the core of VMI. And, as we all know, fifty years ago, women at VMI were visitors from other colleges; today, they make up 11 percent of the corps and are an important segment of the growing number of members of our alumni body.

In national surveys of entering freshmen fifty years ago, the primary reason given by new cadets for choosing VMI was its academic reputation. That remains true today for our increasingly improving academic program that has grown from thirteen to fourteen majors and—more dramatically—from eleven to thirty minors and concentrations. There is now more of a balance among the various majors. Today, the number of cadets majoring in math, science, and engineering stands at a healthy and balanced 58 percent. Another change has been the dramatic expansion of undergraduate research and foreign study programs, ... what former Superintendent Knapp, who significantly strengthened them, always called "VMI's Window on the World."

Since the time of General Shell and General Morgan, the VMI faculty has continued to improve in credentials, to the point that now 100 percent of the full-time faculty in degree-granting departments hold the PhD degree. Small classes—on average a ratio of twelve cadets to one professor—make it possible for these highly qualified and motivated instructors to know their cadets and to provide important personal guidance.

Always a close second to the academic program among the reasons young men and women select VMI has been its military program. The military program has been attractive for two closely related reasons: one is the structure of the regulated military life that it offers, and second is the possibility of a commission in the armed forces, whether duty in the National Guard, Reserve, or Active forces. Two decades ago, the number of cadets choosing to pursue a commission had fallen to 37 percent principally because of the dropping of VMI's policy of mandatory commissioning; currently 57 percent will commission across all services at May graduation. These officers reflect high intelligence, skill, leadership and commitment to the VMI citizen-soldier ideal . . . serving for a short period and moving on to their chosen profession.

One of the greatest changes at VMI over the past decades, as elsewhere, has been the expanded use of computers, cell phones, and other electronic devices. Cadets today have no understanding of slide rules that populated the early sixties. Today, we are a wireless post . . . with the very best high-tech classrooms.

Life in the corps, although very similar to life fifty years ago, has undergone many notable changes. Gone is the five-and-a-half-day academic week, gone is marching to class, gone is a Rat Line that used to continue for most of the academic year. And gone is the "spring hike," replaced with fall and spring Individual Service FTXs. The result I would counter: fewer chiggers and sore feet and greater physicality, discipline, enhanced academics, and more constructive and lasting accomplishments. Even VMI's historic Honor System has changed with the introduction of a jury system; however, it remains a single sanction Honor System, executed by the Corps of Cadets, the only such public college system in the nation.

Perhaps the most evident change in front of us today is the renovation of the physical plant. From a new third barracks, a corps physical training facility, new baseball and other athletic fields, development of North and South Posts, the Center for Leadership and Ethics, a full massive renovation of Cormack Hall and Cocke Hall, and renovation of all major academic buildings and Crozet Hall along Letcher Avenue, and many other significant improvements, we now have a modern physical plant that serves the essential programs . . . and provides the foundation for the VMI educational system. This summer, we will commence a $30 million addition to Scott Shipp Hall, a $15 million modernization of Preston Library, a $30 million upgrade of post infrastructure, and the planning of a $41 million Phase III corps physical training facility (massive aquatic center). VMI and the commonwealth have committed more than $500 million in a decade to this post-transformational effort.

There is much concern nationally these days about the growing deficit in the number of young people who are prepared for STEM jobs in the US, and especially in engineering. According to recent reports, only 16 percent of American high school seniors are proficient in mathematics and interested in STEM careers, with the result that the US ranks 25th in mathematics and 17th in science in the world. We recognized this in 2003 as a "developing" national security issue . . . and, thus, it became one of our major Vision 2039 objectives.

At VMI, it is an interest that we face daily because we are committed to STEM education. Not only does this meet a national need, but it is also true to VMI's historic commitment to science, engineering, and mathematics education that dates back to its founding in 1839. In 2003, at graduation, VMI's degree presentation was 33 percent in the STEM and 67 percent in the pure liberal arts. For over a decade since then, we have worked hard to encourage incoming cadets to enroll in STEM degree programs. Our goal has been 50 percent STEM graduates and 50 percent pure liberal arts graduates "at graduation," thus accounting for attrition and transfers to other majors. This balanced goal has been achieved at a time we (also) significantly grew the Corps of Cadets, and in the face of continuing state financial cuts . . . (from 48 percent of operational budget in 2003 to 14 percent today) . . . and is now holding firm. Why have we . . . did we . . . settle on this balance? In addition to the critical importance of liberal arts majors who go on to careers in business, teaching, foreign service, military, law, and many other professions, including selective medical fields . . . it is also essential that engineers be able to write, present, and communicate proposals, understand history, ethics, and have some knowledge of foreign languages. To make sure this happens, our economics & business, English, history, international studies, modern languages, and other liberal arts departments must be first-rate, taught by the best doctoral instructors. And I can assure you that they are. These same instructors want to graduate cadets into their specialty fields of the arts, foreign affairs, business, and others; they desire to do more than just be a "service department" in support of STEM degrees. We think we have the "right" balance at fifty-fifty that insures a broad liberal arts education . . . and many STEM graduates for the nation . . . and with "impressive" very qualified instructors across our faculty.

The "partnership" programs we have established with large doctoral-research universities continue to enhance our educational experience with cutting-edge instructor currency, intern opportunities for our cadets, and the attainment of master's degrees. We are creating new initiatives to encourage VMI graduates to become instructors at the Institute, and elsewhere, supported by scholarships for attaining a master's degree and designation as "fellows." Our goal is to have several "fellows"—new graduates—per academic department, with the hope that some will continue on to earn the PhD and eventually be selected as permanent members of our faculty.

In sports, we have moved from the Southern Conference to the Big South and back again to the Southern Conference. Today, intercollegiate athletics have become a big business, as we participate in eighteen sports (eleven male and seven female), and it takes special effort and commitment for a small college like VMI to participate and compete, but that is our intention. We believe that althletics are integral to leadership. We complement NCAA sports with a rich international and national competitive club sports program with greater than 60 percent of the corps playing NCAA and club sports.

All across the country, we see that college costs have increased. At VMI, in-state tuition and fees have increased to $27,000 for in-state and to $53,000 for out-of-state students . . . which places the Institute midway on the spectrum of all public colleges in the state. As mentioned earlier, the state's contribution to higher education, through the general fund, has declined, so we have had to be diligent in finding other sources of supplemental funding. It should be noted, however, that the commonwealth's commitment to VMI's Vision 2039, with capital resources, has been remarkable.

Despite the decade-long economic downturn, the shortfall of revenues in the commonwealth and national challenges, I can report that the Institute is flourishing, its reputation is strong, its academic program has never been better, our facilities across the entire post provide an enhanced environment for learning, wellness, and leader development, and our cadets and graduates are impressive.

A major reason for VMI's continued strength and success is, as you know, that the Institute has just completed a wonderful campaign. The campaign was called *An Uncommon Purpose: A Glorious Past, A Brilliant Future: The Campaign for VMI*. In the quiet phase, we selected $180 million as our goal; when we publicly kicked the campaign off in November 2014, because of such early success, we set a new goal of $225 million. The theme of the campaign was deliberately chosen to reflect what makes VMI so unique in today's higher education landscape. We stand for something most other colleges and universities cannot claim, and ensuring this mission continues long into the future was at the heart of the campaign priorities. But I must say, the label of *Uncommon* certainly applied to this campaign effort and the response we received. The campaign officially closed on 30 June 2017 with cash and pledges in excess of $344 million, made possible by 15,000 donors. Thank you for your enormous contribution and support of the Institute and its future.

The future is bright. Vision 2039 continues to be our roadmap.

Yes, since you graduated, much has changed, but much at VMI has remained unchanged. And, in this respect, I am talking about the fundamental ideals and systems that have sustained the Institute throughout its long history. Despite the many changes in the look and fabric of the Institute, it remains essentially what it has always been: a disciplined community of learning and individual development, dedicated to the highest standards of integrity and personal honor.

We continue to teach cadets how to organize, manage time, break down a problem, think under pressure, exercise leadership—and always with honor. These qualities may help to explain why VMI graduates are much in demand by employers, with 99 percent of graduates who seek employment or admission to advanced schools succeeding in their search.

As we reflect back on the class of 1968's time in barracks in the midst of the historical '60s and the fifty years since . . . I hope you agree with me that . . .

Our impressive history, fundamentals, uniqueness, traditions, and alumni are very important. We should execute our daily duties with great care, precision, thought, and the best of judgment . . . and that our values and systems to inculcate them must be secured despite the many pressures of regulatory directives, litigation, social, and other attacks we constantly face.

This is a time for optimism . . . yet . . . great steadiness and resolve! Above all, we must always consider the needs and aspirations of the talented and dedicated young men and women who come here—generation after generation—to prepare for their life's work. In the final analysis, we will be judged by the graduates that we produce, just as VMI has been judged by your outstanding accomplishments and contributions to our nation. I believe the Institute is a national treasure!

I hope you have a memorable reunion. Thank you for your loyal support . . . and welcome back to VMI, the great class of 1968. Please come back with frequency. Good evening.

ACKNOWLEDGMENTS

★ ★ ★

Whenever you conduct a survey, you never know what you will get. So, my first pleasant surprise was that 44 percent of the surviving VMI Class of '68 took the entire survey. The open rate (those who opened the survey) was a bit higher, but I got responses from a few men who said they do not take surveys.

This study would have never come to fruition without the help of the 121 men from the 1968 class who answered my survey. For those who took the time to answer all forty questions, many of which were completely open-ended and required time and thought, I am truly grateful. You made this project a reality.

Gratitude goes to class agent Tom Hickey for helping me contact surviving members of the Class of '68. My husband, Paul Hebert ('68), assisted me with the development of the survey questions, and he reached out to classmates who had not answered, requesting them to find the survey and please answer. He read an unaccountable number of drafts and provided me with details of student life at VMI. I am also grateful to the three men from the Class of '68 who wrote their life stories to enhance this book: John VanLandingham, Creigh Kelley, and Paul Hebert.

Several people read drafts of chapters or the whole book and provided me with valuable information and feedback: Colonel Dean Kershaw ('68), Tom Hickey ('68), Colonel Brad Coleman ('95), Lynn Seldon ('83), VMI Museum Director and historian Keith Gibson, former VMI Dean General Jeffrey Smith ('79), Ed Johnson ('79) of the VMI Alumni Association, SkipRoberts, Todd Goen, VMI director of international students, Colorado historian Arianthe Stettner, Paul's sister-in-law Julie Hebert, and dear friend Helen Dempsey. Dr. Carl Steidtmann and Barbara Sparks gave me valuable feedback on a very early draft. Thanks goes to VMI Superintendent J. H. Binford Peay for allowing me to include his inspiring speech to the Class of 1968 at their 2018 fiftieth reunion. And finally, the VMI archives provided considerable help in finding obscure bits of information.

BIBLIOGRAPHY

* ★ *

Chernow, Ron. 2010. *Washington, A Life*, (New York: The Penguin Press).

Couper, William. 1939. *One Hundred Years at V.M.I.*, Volumes 1-4 (Richmond, Va.: Garrett and Massie Inc.).

Davis, Thomas W. ed., 1988. *A Crowd of Honorable Youths, Historical Essays on the First 150 Years of the Virginia Military Institute*, 145. VMI Sesquicentennial Committee, Lexington, Virginia.

Gibson, Keith A. 2010. *Virginia Military Institute*. (Charlestown, S.C.: Arcadia Publishing).

Green, Kristen. 2015. *Something Must Be Done About Prince Edward County: A Family, a Virginia Town, a Civil Rights Battle* (New York: Harper Collins Publishers).

Hogan, Danny. 2019. *Historical Infrastructure of the Virginia Military Institute and Related Biographies* (Manakin-Sabot, VA: Dementi Milestone Publishing).

Hunter, Robert F. and Edwin L. Dooley Jr. 1989. *Claudius Crozet, French Engineer in America 1790-1864* (Charlottesville: University of Virginia Press).

Horwitz, Tony. 1998. *Confederates in the Attic: Dispatches from the Unfinished Civil War* (New York: Pantheon).

Johnston, J. Eston, ed. 1937. *Echoes of V.M.I. (Lexington, VA: Virginia Military Institute).*

Kanefield, Teri. 2014. *The Girl from the Tar Paper School, Barbara Rose Johns and the Advent of the Civil Rights Movement* (New York: Abrams).

Mann, Charles C. 2011. *1493: Uncovering the New World Columbus Created* (New York: Alfred A. Knopf).

Miller, Jonson. 2020. *Engineering Manhood: Race and the Antebellum Virginia Military Institute*. (Lever Press). https://www.jstor.org/stable/10.3998/mpub.11675767.5.

Seidule, Ty. 2020. *Robert E. Lee and Me—A Southerner's Reckoning with the Myth of the Lost Cause* (New York: St. Martin's Press).

Schaffner, Randolph P. 2014. *The Father of VMI: A Biography of Colonel J.T.L. Preston* (Jefferson, NC: McFarland and Company).

Wise, Henry A. 1978. *Drawing Out the Man: the VMI Story* (Charlottesville: University Press of Virginia).

Woodward, Colin. 2011. *American Nations: A History of the Eleven Rival Regional Cultures of North America* (New York: Penguin Books).

Woodward, Colin. 2017. *American Character: A History of the Epic Struggle Between Individual Liberty and the Common Good.* (New York: Penguin Books).

ENDNOTES

* * *

1. Britannica. 2023. "Lost Cause." https://www.britannica.com/topic/Lost-Cause.
2. Deetz et al. 2016. "Redefining History and Heritage at Virginia's Colleges and Universities," History News, Autumn 2016, Vol. 71. No. 4, pp. 26-31. https://www.jstor.org/stable/44605958.
3. Virginia Military Institute. 2023. "Operating Rules of the Institute Schedule, General Order Number 01, 23 February 2023." https://www.vmi.edu/media/content-assets/documents/general-orders/GO1.pdf.
4. Virginia Military Institute - Catalog.vmi.edu. 2021. Dismissal and Other Penalties. https://www.vmi.edu/media/content-assets/documents/registrar/VMI-Catalogue-2021-2022.pdf.
5. Virginia Military Institute - Office of the Commandant. 2013. *The Bullet*: The RAT BIBLE for the Rat Mass of the 2013."
6. VMI 1968 *Commencement Exercises* booklet, June 9, 1968.
7. VanLandingham, John. 2022. Personal Communication.
8. VanLandingham, John. 2022.
9. The Saturday Evening Post. 1939. "Men of Courage." https://www.bing.com/images/search?view=detailV2&ccid=qZIMbzSR&id
10. Couper, William. 1939. *One Hundred Years at VMI*, Vol. 1 (Richmond: Garrett and Massey, Inc.).
11. Wise, Henry A. 1978. *Drawing Out the Man: The VMI Story* (Charlottesville: University Press of Virginia).
12. Gibson, Keith A. 2010. *Virginia Military Institute*. (Charlestown, S.C.: Arcadia Publishing).
13. Hogan, Danny. 2019. *Historical Infrastructure of the Virginia Military Institute and Related Biographies* (Manakin-Sabot, VA: Dementi Milestone Publishing).
14. Miller, Jonson. 2020. *Engineering Manhood: Race and the Antebellum Virginia Military Institute* (Lever Press). https://www.jstor.org/stable/10.3998/mpub.11675767.5.

15. Hunter, Robert F. and Edwin L. Dooley Jr. 1989. *Claudius Crozet, French Engineer in America 1790-1864* (Charlottesville: University of Virginia Press).
16. Shaffner, Randolph P. 2014. *The Father of VMI: A Biography of Colonel J.T.L. Preston* (Jefferson, NC: McFarland and Company).
17. Woodward, Colin. 2017. *American Character: A History of the Epic Struggle Between Individual Liberty and the Common Good, 69.* (New York: Penguin Books).
18. Woodward. 2017, 70.
19. Chernow, Ron. 2010. *Washington, A Life,* 63. (New York: The Penguin Press).
20. Mount Vernon.org. 2022. "Ten Facts about George Washington and the French and Indian War." https://www.mountvernon.org/george-washington/french-indian-war/ten-facts-about-george-washington-and-the-french-indian-war/.
21. Chernow. 2010, 39-62.
22. Chernow. 2010, 91.
23. Chernow. 2010, 92.
24. Founders Online. 2022. "Address from the Officers of the Virginia Regiment, 31 December 1758." https://founders.archives.gov/documents/Washington/02-06-02-0147.
25. Woodward, Colin. 2011. *American Nations: A History of the Eleven Rival Regional Cultures of North America* (New York: Penguin Books).
26. Miller. 2020.
27. Mann, Charles C. 2011. *1493: Uncovering the New World Columbus Created,* 332. (New York: Alfred A. Knopf)
28. Mountvernon.org. 2022. "10 Facts About Washington & Slavery." www.mountvernon.org.
29. Monticello.org. 2022. "Jefferson & Slavery." 2022. www.monticello.org.
30. Monticello.org. 2022. "Jefferson's Attitudes Toward Slavery." www.monticello.org.
31. *Encyclopedia Virginia.* 2023."Gabriel's Conspiracy." https://encyclopediavirginia.org/entries/gabriels-conspiracy-1800/.
32. National Park Service. 2023. "Denmark Vesey." https://www.nps.gov/people/denmark-vesey.htm.
33. Britannica. 2023. "Nat Turner." https://www.britannica.com/biography/.
34. Miller. 2020. 81.
35. Miller. 2020. 228-229.

36. Miller. 2020.
37. Miller. 2020.
38. Couper, William. 1939. *One Hundred Years at V.M.I.*, Volume 1. (Richmond, Va.: Garrett and Massie Inc.).
39. Hunter and Dooley. 1989.
40. Southall, James P. C. 1936. "Richard Cocke of Bremo and His Children." *The Virginia Magazine of History and Biography* 44, no. 2 (1936): 136–51. http://www.jstor.org/stable/4244720.
41. Klepper, Michael and Robert Gunther. 1996. *The Wealthy 100: From Benjamin Franklin to Bill Gates—a Ranking of the Richest Americans, Past and Present*, 205-207. (New York: Citadel Press).
42. Koons, Kenneth & *Dictionary of Virginia Biography*. 2020. "Philip St. George Cocke (1809–1861)." (2020, December 07). In *Encyclopedia Virginia*. https://encyclopediavirginia.org/entries/cocke-philip-st-george-1809-1861.
43. VMI Archives Digital Collections. 2023. "Philip St. Geroge Cocke." Virginia Military Institute https://archivesweb.vmi.edu/rosters/record.php?ID=11659.
44. VMI Archives Official Records. 2023. "VMI Superintendents Since 1839." https://www.vmi.edu/archives/vmi-official-records/vmi-superintendents-since-1839/.
45. Keith Gibson, personal communication
46. VMI Archives Catalogue. 2023. "Cocke, William H. (William Horner), 1874–1938." https://archivesspace.vmi.edu/agents/people/1419.
47. Read, Beverly R. 1988. "Sculpture at VMI: Statues and Other Heroic Works of Art," in *A Crowd of Honorable Youths: Historical Essays on the first 150 Years of Virginia Military Institute*, edited by Thomas W. Davis (Lexington, VA: Virginia Military Institute).
48. Keith Gibson, VMI Museum Director, personal communication, June 2020.
49. Keith Gibson, personal communication.
50. Fine Art Investigations. 2023. William James Hubard (1807-1862). https://fineartinvestigations.com/artists/hubard/.
51. Hogan. 2019. 61.
52. Marr, Robert A. 1937. "V.M.I. in the Civil War," in *Echoes of V.M.I*, 13, edited by J. Eston Johnston, (Virginia Military Institute).
53. Biography. 2023. "John Brown." www.biography.com/activist/john-brown.

54 John M. McClure. 2014. "Edmund Ruffin (1794–1865)," in *Encyclopedia Virginia*, January 4, 2014. http://www.EncyclopediaVirginia.org/Ruffin_Edmund_1794-1865.

55 Green, Jennifer R. 2015. "Virginia Military Institute during the Civil War," in *Encyclopedia Virginia*, October 27, 2015. http://www.EncyclopediaVirginia.org/Virginia_Military_Institute_During_the_Civil_War.

56 Gibson, Keith, 2021. personal communication.

57 Green. Jennifer R. 2015. "Virginia Military Institute during the Civil War."

58 National Park Service. 2023. "Edmund Ruffin." https://www.nps.gov/people/edmund-ruffin.htm.

59 VMI Archives Digital Collections. 2021. "Historical Rosters Database." https://archivesweb.vmi.edu/rosters/index.php.

60 Mann. 2011. *260–261*.

61 VMI Archives. 2023. "VMI in Civil War FAQ." https://www.vmi.edu/archives/manuscripts/new-market--vmi-in-the-civil-war/vmi-in-civil-war-faq/.

62 Green, Jennifer. 2015. "Virginia Military Institute during the Civil War."

63 National Park Service 2023. "Edmund Ruffin."

64 Southern Poverty Law Center. 2019. "Whose Heritage? Public Symbols of the Confederacy." https://www.splcenter.org/20190201/whose-heritage-public-symbols-confederacy.

65 VMI Archives. 2023. "New Market Ceremony History." https://www.vmi.edu/archives/civil-war-and-new-market/battle-of-new-market/new-market-ceremony-history/.

66 Seck, Hope Hodge. 2022. "What to do with Arlington Cemetery's Confederate Memorial," *The Washington Post*, December 30, 2022.

67 Southern Poverty Law Center. 2019.

68 VMI Archives. 2023. "Statues and monuments at VMI." https://www.vmi.edu/archives/vmi-archives-faqs/statues-and-monuments-at-vmi/.

69 Gill, John Freeman. 2023. "How Six Italian Brothers Shaped the Story of New York." *The New York Times*, October 15, 2023.

70 Ask Art. 2023. "Attilio Piccirilli (1866–1945)." https://www.askart.com/artist/Attilio_Piccirilli/70968/Attilio_Piccirilli.aspx.

71 VMI Museum. n.d. *Memorial Garden* (VMI Museum leaflet). Virginia Military Institute, Lexington, Virginia.

72 Read, Beverly M. 1988. 145.

73 Virginia Military Institute. 2022. VMI Annual Awards Program Policy. General Order Number 76, 28 September 2022, Virginia Military Institute, 3. https://www.vmi.edu/media/content-assets/documents/general-orders/GO76.pdf.

74 Deetz et al. 2016

75 Gibson, 2021. personal communication.

76 Sonnenburg, Rhonda. 2022. "Under Attack: Virginia Military Institute's Culture is Forced to Change – But How Much?" Southern Poverty Law Center, June 17, 2022. www.splcenter.org.

77 VMI Annual Awards Program Policy, 2022. General Order Number 76, 7.

78 The Cadet newspaper. 2023. "Reinstatement of Moses Ezekiel Award." *The Cadet*, 28 April 2023. https://cadetnewspaper.com/news/489/reinstatement-of-moses-ezekiel-award.

79 Conrad Wharton. 2013. "The New Market Cadet Legacy Award." *The Cadet*, October 4, 2013. VMI Archives. https://digitalcollections.vmi.edu/digital/collection/p15821coll8/id/24748/rec/2.

80 General J. H. Binford Peay, III Superintendent. 2018. "1968—A Momentous Year in US History - remarks at the fiftieth Reunion of the class of 1968, Marshall Hall, April 20, 2018."

81 Matthew Twombly. 2018. "A Timeline of 1968: The Year That Shattered America," *Smithsonian Magazine, January–February 2018*. https://www.smithsonianmag.com/history/timeline-seismic-180967503/.

82 Garfield, Leanna and Zoe Ettinger. 2020. "14 of the biggest marches and protests in American history." *Business Insider*, June 1, 2020. https://www.businessinsider.com.

83 History.com. 2023. "Vietnam War: Dates and Timeline." https://www.history.com/topics/vietnam-war.

84 Virginia Military Institute. 2018. "Heroism, Resilience, and Sacrifice on Display." September 20, 2018. https://www.vmi.edu/news/headlines/2018-2019/heroism-resilience-and-sacrifice-on-display.php.

85 Tom Garner. 2016. "Vietnam War Songs: What Happened When the Beatles Met Bertrand Russell," *History of War*, January 19, 2016. https://www.historyanswers.co.uk/history-of-war/vietnam-war-songs-what-happened-when-the-beatles-met-bertrand-russell/.

86 Teri Kanefield. 2014. *The Girl from the Tar Paper School, Barbara Rose Johns and the Advent of the Civil Rights Movement, 10.* (New York: Abrams).

87. Longwood University Students-Moton Museum, Joint Venture. 2014. *10 Stories 50 Years Later*, Vol. 1., Ed. 3, Spring 2014, Prince Edward County Virginia.
88. Moton Museum-Longwood University students, Joint Venture. 2018. *All Eyes on Prince Edward County.* Vol. 3, Ed.2, Spring 2018, Farmville, Va.
89. Green, Kristin. 2015. *Something Must Be Done About Prince Edward County: A Family, a Virginia Town, a Civil Rights Battle* (New York: Harper Collins Publishers).
90. Mattingly, Justin. 2018. "'We Were No Different': Virginia Military Institute Integrated 50 Years Ago," *Richmond Times-Dispatch*, December 20, 2018.
91. Finn, Peter. 1997. "At VMI, Pioneers Recall Breaking Earlier Barrier," *Washington Post, October 5, 1997.*
92. US Government, 2021. "45th Anniversary of Women Admitted to West Point." www.govinfo.gov.This font looks smaller than others.
93. Seidule, Ty. 2020. *Robert E. Lee and Me—A Southerner's Reckoning with the Myth of the Lost Cause, 108.* (New York: St. Martin's Press).
94. Horwitz, Tony. 1998. *Confederates in the Attic: Dispatches from the Unfinished Civil War, 270.* (New York: Pantheon).
95. Barnes & Thornburg LLP. 2021. "Marching Toward Inclusive Excellence: An Equity Audit and Investigation of the Virginia Military Institute." Final Report of the Barnes & Thornburg LLP Special Investigation Team, June 1, 2021.
96. Marina Sohma. 2016. "The Oldest Usable Bridge in the World Was Built by 70,000 Roman Prisoners." Ancient Origins. https://www.ancient-origins.net/ancient-places-asia/dezful-bridge-oldest-usable-bridge-world-was-built-70000-roman-prisoners-006995.
97. Robert Seamus Macpherson. 2021. *Stewards of Humanity—Lighting the Darkness in Humanitarian Crisis.* (Durham, NC: Torchflame Books).
98. Gibson. 2010, 7.
99. VMI Alumni Association. 2023. Personal Communication, March 2023.

SURVEY QUESTIONS

★ ★ ★

- ★ Where did you graduate from high school?
- ★ Why did you choose to go to VMI?
- ★ What was your major?
- ★ Did you earn a postgraduate degree?
- ★ What degree did you pursue?
- ★ Did you obtain the degree?
- ★ What profession or professions did you pursue in your life? (mark all that apply)
- ★ Were you happy with your chosen profession?
- ★ Did VMI prepare you well for your postgraduate education or profession?
- ★ If not well prepared, in what ways unprepared?
- ★ What are the different places you lived in your life after leaving VMI? (states or countries)
- ★ Where do you live now?
- ★ What branch of the military did you serve in?
- ★ How long did you serve in the military?
- ★ Were you ever in combat?
- ★ Where did you serve in combat?
- ★ What was your highest military rank?
- ★ What life lessons did you learn from military service?
- ★ What life lessons did you learn from your career?
- ★ Did you ever marry?
- ★ Did you marry your Ring Figure date?
- ★ What year did you marry?
- ★ How long did your first marriage last?
- ★ How many times have you married?
- ★ What reasons would you give for a marriage lasting?

- ★ What reasons would you give for a marriage ending?
- ★ What lessons did you learn from your marriage?
- ★ Have you had any mental health issues such as PTSD, alcoholism, drug addiction, sex addiction, food addiction, pornography, or gambling? Did you overcome it?
- ★ If so, how did you overcome it?
- ★ How many children did you have (natural and adopted)?
- ★ Did any of your children attend VMI?
- ★ What are the most wonderful things that happened in your life?
- ★ What did you learn from the wonderful things that happened in your life?
- ★ What are the worst things that happened in your life?
- ★ What lessons did you learn from the worst things that happened in your life?
- ★ What advice would you give VMI to better prepare students or life?

www.ingramcontent.com/pod-product-compliance
Lightning Source LLC
LaVergne TN
LVHW041912070526
838199LV00051BA/2594